Heroes in the Halls

The Book on Recognizing
The Leader Within You

Claude Halpin

ISBN: 978-1-77277-062-9

PUBLISHED BY:
10-10-10 PUBLISHING
MARKHAM, ON
CANADA

Contents

Acknowledgements

Many thanks to my dear wife Heather, who has been a source of energy and support, during the months writing this book.

To my friends and colleagues: Tom Schonberg, President and CEO of the Queensway Carleton Hospital, Ottawa, Ontario; David Montgomery, President and CEO of the Haldimand War Memorial Hospital, Dunnville, Ontario; Phil Watkins, Business Manager, the Vanier Centre for Women; Donald Witchell, President of Synergex, Toronto, Ontario, for their reviews and comments on sections of this book "Heroes in the Halls."

Particular thanks to the nine outstanding "Heroes" who contributed to the spirit of the book. They all agreed to an extensive interview designed to determine what motivated and inspired them to become exemplary employees and leaders.

The nine came from small and large community hospitals, major teaching hospitals, a mental health center, a public health agency and a private sector long-term care organization.

These "Heroes" represent the excellence of thousands of employees caring for patients and residents across Canada.

"Heroes in the Halls" was written to help the best become better through an increased understanding of the basic principles of management. The book shows how employees can become future participants in assisting their leaders through an increased understanding of the managerial and human demands their leaders face every day.

Testimonials

"Claude's insightful book is for anyone who works in health care, at all levels. Through his wisdom and helpful real life examples, he inspires the leader, the emerging leader, and those who have not yet considered their leadership potential, to take their careers to the next level and beyond. Claude reminds us that, despite all the challenges that exist in any health system, there is every reason for hope and optimism. Our patients and residents are counting on it."

David Montgomery, President and CEO
Haldimand War Memorial Hospital
Dunnville, Ontario, Canada

"There is little doubt that every health care employee is a "Hero" in some respect. Claude has captured in this book profiles of several diverse "Heroes' who are highly motivated, love what they do and constantly contribute to excellence within their departments and organizations. A summary of their inputs, numbering 25, is captured in this book and will benefit all staff and their leaders in stimulating personal reflection. The book also describes "Principles of Management" which can be used by staff to benefit interactions with leaders, peers and their families. This book "Heroes in the Halls" is easy to understand and a practical collection of role models to stimulate the potential of our people, increase engagement and improve care for those we serve within our organizations across Canada."

Tom Schonberg, President and CEO
Queensway Carleton Hospital
Ottawa, Ontario, Canada

"I have had the pleasure to read Claude Halpin's "Heroes in the Halls" book. It is an inspiring read that highlights the unsung heroes we work with every day. As a senior manager it has provided me with some insightful tips on how better to engage my staff and make them heroes in my organization. A must read for both new and seasoned managers."

Philip J. Watkins, CPA, CGA and Business Manager
Vanier Centre for Women
Milton, Ontario, Canada

"Heroes in the Halls" is a must read for employees of hospitals and all healthcare organizations. It features the results of interviews with 9 "Heroes" describing their philosophies and motivations, to improve their organizations and delivery of patient care. The "Heroes" book describes the "Principles of Management" that guide their leaders every day and that every staff member can use at both home and work to improve their lives in many areas like coping with stress, change and effective communication. This book is designed to release the potential of every employee through increased understanding of their leaders, teambuilding, and improved services at all organizational levels. If only I had this book at the start of my career."

Don Witchell, President
Synergex Performance Enhancement Inc.
Toronto, Ontario, Canada

Foreword

When you think of a hero, what image comes to mind? You are probably envisioning a powerful, muscular man or woman soaring through the sky, with a cape billowing behind. After all, isn't that what the stories taught you at an early age about heroes?

But now, put your image aside for a moment. Ask yourself, what characteristics do you envision heroes to have, instead of what they look like? Would you say leadership? Courage? Caring? Like the image you conjured, these are the values most people think of when considering heroism. But here's what's interesting: while you aren't Superman or Superwoman, you do have many qualities and talents that can make you a hero too. You just need the tools to unleash them.

In Heroes in the Halls, Claude Halpin, an expert in health care management, carefully explains these tools. During his career he has held several executive leadership roles in Canada, including three CEO positions in Health Centres ranging from 290 to 2500 beds. Moreover, the education he brings to his job is extensive and varied. If you were to ask Claude what to him is a real hero, he would tell you that heroes are great communicators, they are empathetic, positive, and truly love people. Heroes take on the role in health care as they care for their colleagues and strive to help you become a true hero.

The qualities Claude has identified as inherent in a hero are clear. He includes the ones you already see as important and apparent, and then he takes it a step further. He demonstrates how less obvious traits are indicative of a hero, such as teamwork, planning, setting goals and attaining them. Even better, he provides you with real-life examples of heroes in the halls. Most impactful of all, are the clearly defined steps Claude provides to teach you how to be a hero, and how to recognize the many heroes you encounter daily. Finally, he teaches you how to successfully incorporate the heroism of staff at any level in a manner that creates a strong and successful working environment.

Raymond Aaron
New York Bestselling Author

Introduction

This book is unique in that it is based on the author's 40 years of leadership experience in the health care field as a CEO, officer, educator and consultant. It recognizes that almost one million Canadians and millions of Americans are employed in health care, long-term care, public health and a wide range of social service agencies and organizations.

The book is written to provide education, insights and guidance for all levels of staff related to the concepts and practices of management and leadership that make our organizations operate. It is crafted to enable the reader to understand various principles of management and leadership. It demonstrates how anyone can use these principles to become better informed, become leaders themselves, and use several principles such as change, stress and communications to be more effective members of their departments while improving all family and personal relationships.

"Heroes in the Halls" recognizes that every hour of every day, and every day of every year, there are hundreds of thousands of men and women caring for millions of individuals requiring care and personal services ranging from the most complex surgical procedures such as cardiac and neurosurgery, to a wide range of therapeutic and general services designed to restore individuals to healthier and improved lives.

We have in our health systems thousands of physicians in all branches of medicine. We have sophisticated university affiliated teaching hospitals, and community general hospitals serving the bulk of our communities. We have small hospitals in the far north of our country—some with less than 10 beds—all caring for our diverse publics.

Every health care or caring organization requires an army of general and specialized staff, to care for employees, staff and organizational needs ranging from food services to housekeeping, to environmental services, clerical staff and security.

These are our "Heroes" —they always have been and always will be. Our leadership teams must recognize their contributions and develop practices that will allow every hero to contribute to improved patient care and in turn their personal lives.

It is hard to believe that we have so much raw talent within our organizations, waiting to be unleashed by progressive leaders.

This book is designed to change our organizations by recognizing and utilizing the potential of the human power we have within our structures so as to improve everything we do personally and organizationally.

The following pages, and chapters, will take the reader through a journey that will not be forgotten, as we review the demands of organizational life and how we must support the teams we work with, as we become leaders ourselves.

We'll learn how to deal with complexities, how to deal with stress and how to cope with never-ending change. We will learn how to be happy, proud and trusting staff members. We'll learn about the power of visualization and how we can use that skill to provide ourselves with a way of successfully handling our future challenges, both departmentally and personally.

Learning the Facts of Organizational Life at the University of Toronto

During my second year of graduate work at the University of Toronto I had the distinct privilege to spend a residency year at one of Toronto's and Canada's finest teaching hospitals - The Toronto Western Hospital. I learned more in that one year residency than you would normally in ten years working in a hospital.

Our program was designed to have each resident follow a careful schedule, and visit and study every department, and service, in the hospital—we were learning the business and skills of Health Care.

During that year I learned how every department operated, how patients were cared for, and viewed autopsies, the births of babies, the activities of a busy emergency department, the functions of rehabilitation medicine, the science of complex laboratories and most significantly how hospital staffs must operate as teams to provide the highest quality care for their patients.

A Lesson in Teamwork

During one of my visits to an operating room at the Toronto Western I had the opportunity of observing one of Ontario's most skilled thoracic (chest) surgeons complete the removal of a lung from a middle-aged gentleman.

The left side of the patient's chest was wide open, waiting to be closed by the specialist. The surgery had resulted in bleeding and the surgeon was starting to use a device to cauterize the many "bleeders" that required attention. Suddenly, the surgeon looked up and said, "We have a problem."

At that instant the Senior Operating Room Nurse came to the OR table, picked up and disconnected the cautery and left the room. She returned a minute later with a new cautery, connected it and passed it to the surgeon who finished his work. This action probably saved the patient's life.

So why am I telling you this? And why have I told the story to hundreds of classes in management and leadership? It is simply to illustrate that, no matter who you are and how talented and experienced you might be, everyone must rely on others for their successes in hospitals.

Throughout this book, we will be illustrating how we are dependent on others no matter what we do. The joy and happiness associated with working together can contribute to your satisfaction and meaning of life—it is something we should never forget. We will discuss how we can create outstanding teams in the future—any employee can lead groups—we'll discuss how.

Chapter One
The Stories of Our Heroes

"Heroes in the Halls" was written in recognition of the fact that most general staff members within health care facilities have little opportunity to learn about the principles of management and how management works in general. Everyone is responsible to a supervisor, manager, or director who provides leadership and employee guidance. This system works, but it can be enhanced through sharing the concepts of management through staff education and studying this book. By exposing our staff to a number of traditional management concepts they will become more understanding of the responsibilities of their managers. At the same time, they will be able to use their new knowledge to become greater contributors to their departments and organizations.

In addition to the work setting, this new information provided by our heroes allows staff members to assist their own families in many activities, including effective planning, communicating and stress reduction.

We have so much unused talent to develop within our organizations that it will be possible to make major improvements in everything we do by including all staff as part of their own futures. The individual employee knows what is to be done to make their department or service more effective and harmonious. Progressive management must allow them to become part of the change process through skills described within this "Heroes" publication.

Finding Our Heroes

Of the nine heroes described in this book, six were identified personally based on my observations of them in various work settings. Three heroes were recommended by colleagues; Chief Executive Officers who, with their teams, identified outstanding staff members for inclusion in the book. All nine heroes are health care workers from different organizations and departments and felt honored to contribute their stories to this book.

Interview Processes

All interviews were conducted using a customized questionnaire designed to obtain information on several areas of the work of each hero, including their motivation, involvement, concerns, job satisfaction and some of their day-to-day practices. All participants provided invaluable information regarding factors that kept them highly motivated, patient-focused and satisfied with their work. Brief reviews of the outcome of each interview are described throughout the book.

Lessons Learned

The heroes described in this book provided the author with exceptional information on what makes employees outstanding, respected and in general totally satisfied with who they are and what they do.

Eight of the heroes were interviewed in person, and confidentially for more than an hour. One was interviewed by telephone. They were interviewed at their home facility or center, and were asked to respond to a wide range of questions developed for the process.

All responses were sincere and told of their commitment to their patients, residents and organizations. They were very satisfied with their roles and what they did—they displayed, and described, a sincere interest in those they served and cared for. Just being in the presence of these heroes one could feel their pride and willingness to constantly improve everything they did.

After completing all interviews and meetings, brief reports were written, highlighting all interviews. The briefings are located as a preface to each chapter and are presented for the readers to enjoy as they proceed to read any specific chapter of the book.

Leadership Lessons from our Heroes

After analyzing all interview reports, the following themes or common factors emerged for consideration, and guidance of the reader:

1. Heroes love their work and are enthusiastic.

2. They sincerely care for their patients and are dedicated to them.

3. Those working nearest to, or performing, any job usually know more about that particular job than anyone else.

4. They are anxious to contribute to the continuous improvement of the quality of care provided, and internal departmental relationships.

5. They will collaborate as colleagues and be prepared for activities that will enable them to make direct suggestions for making their departments and operations more effective.

6. They would welcome being asked to use their knowledge and personal abilities to assist with, and plan for, the futures of their departments.

7. Heroes believe that what they give always comes back to them.

8. Most "Heroes" believe in the "Golden Rule:" "Do unto others as you would have them do unto you."

9. Recognition of all staff is essential by managers and each other—we thrive on our successes and appreciate positive feedback at any time.

10. Teams should meet together at regular times for planning and team building activities. either as small groups or departments.

11. All staff can contribute to departmental or organizational planning for the future, once invited by management to participate.

12. Every employee should have goals and objectives to ensure their personal progress and future successes.

13. Every member of staff and every colleague should be treated with respect by their leaders and fellow staff members.

14. Departmental goal setting should occur regularly.

15. General staff education and development programs should occur to benefit the employee at work, and in their home environment.

16. "Heroes" welcome visits to their departments or service areas, and the opportunity of speaking with their leadership team members.

17. Team members often develop their own means for settling departmental disputes.

18. All new employees should be assigned to a mentor, or "buddy," to orientate and help them early in their new assignments, and to assist them in becoming comfortable and knowledgeable about their new environment.

19. Every employee working in a health care setting should be thinking constantly "How can I make the lives of my patients and residents more rewarding?"

20. It is important that managers and supervisors have a thorough understanding of the complexities of each job performed by their staff.

21. There would be value in having all staff, through careful scheduling, visit and observe other areas of their organizations to get a broader perspective of the organization and gain understanding of how all components interrelate and influence each other.

22. Group meetings or brainstorming activities should be encouraged to use team talents to resolve current issues.

23. Staff should be encouraged to develop and use personal or departmental checklists to track repetitive activities and improve efficiency.

24. Managers can receive considerable assistance from their staff by allowing them to work in small groups to develop solutions for departmental issues.

25. The power within our employees is beyond belief--our managers must develop and encourage that environment of participation and involvement.

CHAPTER HIGHLIGHTS

- Significant opportunities exist within the general staff of all Health Care organizations to contribute to problem identification, and resolution, to improve quality care and levels of trust, while encouraging teamwork and team building.

- Through understanding the basic principles of management, staff can learn the roles of their managers, identifying ways to support them in carrying out their leadership responsibilities.

- The 9 "Heroes" profiled in this book are reflective of hundreds of thousands of their colleagues across Canada, all dedicated to serving their patients, residents and organizations.

- The 25 items mentioned under the heading "Leadership Lessons from our Heroes", is a blueprint for leadership and staff to consider, and implement, as appropriate within their departments and organizations.

- Staff need personal recognition and support by leaders at all organizational levels. The challenge is for these leaders to implement practices which will encourage employees to use their full potential to create exemplary departments, and organizations.

Profiles of Our Heroes in the Halls

DORIS

Our hero, Doris, works for a home care organization, which operates as part of a large governmental organization in Southern Alberta. The organization's basic mandate has recently undergone major restructuring. About 65 nurses, including Registered Nurses, Licensed Practical Nurses (LPNs) and Home Support Aides, are part of her team.

This hero has been in the nursing industry for 30 years, loves working with her colleagues, her workload in general, and being an advocate for the elderly clientele she serves. She enjoys her long-term association with elderly persons and is dedicated to making their lives as pleasant as possible.

She frequently is in contact and offers her advice on how best to care for family members. Doris explained that the service must operate in a flexible manner due to the fact that the staff are constantly on the road visiting clients in different communities throughout their catchment area.

Recognition

Recognition comes primarily from those she serves and has a long-term relationship with. She feels like a member of their families, who rely heavily on her for advice and care. Nurse's Week was celebrated recently. Doris and all of her colleagues were presented with red roses as a gesture of appreciation by their manager. After years of dramatic change in Alberta, Doris feels that everything is settling down and improving in general.

Team Building Practices/Approaches/Goal Setting

Team building occurs every day when staff members meet early each morning to communicate, review schedules, receive information from management and then proceed to visit clients. A more formal meeting for all staff is held once each month for planning, government announcements and general issue resolution.

Teamwork is developed early with any new staff members through a "buddy system" which involves an experienced member of staff working with a new person to explain to them the organization, policies, practices, etc. The relationship lasts for several months until the new employee is thoroughly trained and fully aware of the agency's operations.

Planning and goal setting for the Home Care Team is determined provincially and transmitted across the province.

Doris commented that everyone on her team gets along well and that conflicts are resolved quickly. The team members offer to assist each other should the members have available time that could be utilized by serving other clients.

This vital service provides social workers on the team, and the nurses, the opportunity to be assisted by support aids. These aids, in turn, allow some nursing tasks to be delegated to individuals with different levels of training, thereby freeing up professional nursing time. Doris mentioned that different educational courses are scheduled during the year and staff may select those that are interesting to them personally.

Home care services will grow exponentially in the future and continue to become a major area of health care moving forward. We are fortunate to have organizations such as the one described by this "Hero" now operating and preparing for the dramatic expansion of the elderly population in future years.

ANA

Ana is the manager of a large service department providing housekeeping, laundry and maintenance services for a large nursing home-long term care organization in a city near Toronto, Ontario.

Ana has worked in the health care field for over 30 years, "loves" what she does and is very proud of her department and every member of staff. She guides and assists her staff continuously, and is a highly visible leader, touring her facility and keeping in personal contact with her team members and other colleagues every day. In case of emergencies she works with her team personally until the situation is corrected. Other factors that have made her a "hero" to so many over the years are her bubbling personality, her smile, openness and constant enthusiasm. She shares her knowledge with her colleagues, is an excellent listener, compliments her staff and thanks them regularly for their excellent work.

Ana has the greatest respect for the residents she and her staff serve, and spends considerable time with them as she tours her facility.

Recognition

All heroes interviewed were asked to described how they have been recognized by management for their efforts over the years. Ana is satisfied with the recognition she has been given but acknowledged that some leaders were more committed to complimenting their staff than others. Recognition leads to individual motivation, which is a critical element within any organization. Ana herself is very cognizant of this reality and provides regular feedback to her team members.

Team Building Practices/Interaction/Goal Setting

Ana's team meets monthly to generate new ideas, resolve issues, etc. Due to constant work load demands she finds it impossible to meet with them more frequently, so most communications occur during the work day on a one-to-one basis. She commits herself to a "no surprises" environment with her staff, and invites them to always be in touch in case of problems or situations requiring attention.

It was noted that goal and objective setting could be further developed. The department carries out and supports overall corporate strategic goals but has not had time to develop departmental operational goals—this should change in the future.

Team Independence

Under Ana's guidance, her team is empowered to complete their tasks in a professional manner. All members are well aware of their responsibilities and are expected to perform well, and disputes are settled quickly and amicably. There is a commitment within the department to respect everyone and make them feel important. All staff are dedicated to those they serve and the tasks they perform, and there is significant respect for everyone associated with the organization.

CATHERENE

Catherene has worked for 17 years in a major community hospital in the Ottawa area. She is a team leader in acute medicine. The facility has grown from a small community organization to a large several hundred bed sophisticated health care facility. During this time she has been fortunate to work in a number of nursing units from which she gained considerable experience in many facets of nursing.

She prides herself in knowing many staff personally and knows where to go to find answers when she has to. Catherene assumes ownership of everything she does and is committed to becoming a strong leader. She believes that every person wants to do a good job and, when treated with respect, has the ability to provide input and ideas to improve any area of the organization.

Recognition

Catherene is very proud of the fact that she has won a Service Excellence Award, with the hospital acknowledging her continuous high-quality work, patient care standards and basic leadership skills.

The leadership of Catherene's hospital is progressive and committed to staff recognition programs on a continuous basis. Her organization utilizes the LEAN methodology, which is a sophisticated and continuous quality improvement system, producing impressive early results in her facility. As part of overall team recognition and as part of the LEAN system, all involved staff meet or "huddle" for 15 minutes every day to discuss issues, possible areas of service quality improvement, resolve problems and most of all to communicate and listen to each other. Senior management team members also attend these meeting to ensure that they are involved and aware of what is happening within their teams and departments.

Team Building Practices/Approaches/Goal Setting

Catherene explained that all activities within her hospital are based on team involvement. The LEAN system is the driving force for positive change, and is being implemented throughout the hospital with total organizational commitment. Standard work practices are developed and laid out in daily schedules including checklists. Four, Continuous Improvement Officers are available to assist staff and monitor outputs as the system is implemented.

A feature of the process, which is very positive, is that at a predetermined time each day multidisciplinary teams, including physicians, and the primary care nurse, come together for one hour to review the events of the previous 24 hours. This regular dialogue encourages team understanding, and facilitation of patient care, it also enables physicians to meet multidisciplinary team members caring for their specific patients. The practice ensures a continuous treatment and care planning process for every patient on the Unit and is very helpful for discharge planning with the whole team in one area to provide their input. The team finds the physician rounds very beneficial every day.

Planning and goal setting occurs during these times, too. The LEAN System will eventually be implemented within all areas of the hospital. Currently, it is operating in several nursing areas with excellent results. Catherene explains that since the system involves major changes for individuals and their practices, adequate time must be allowed for staff to adapt to and then practice this consistently-applied quality improvement system.

Catherene feels that she works within a very trusting environment where senior management, including the hospital President, who is a full participant and supporter of the LEAN system, frequently attends and contributes his ideas at the meetings. This progressive organization encourages extensive coaching of staff, by their managers and colleagues, and through specific educational programs.

JOELLE

Joelle has worked for a large mental health sciences center in eastern Ontario for approximately seven years. She is a highly regarded member of the environmental services housekeeping staff and is currently working part-time, reporting to a manager/supervisor of this 70-person department. She is an enthusiastic staff member who loves her work, the patients, and the colleagues she works with, and she particularly enjoys working with the youth and the elderly patients cared for at the center. Part of her job entails working closely with the nursing staff and communicating with them regularly.

Joelle has loved cleaning and keeping things neat ever since she was a little girl. Even in school, she was the student who volunteered to help keep the classroom neat, tidy, and well-organized. Her cheerful nature and enthusiasm is contagious and she finds it hard to understand why some staff are not happy with the work they do and their work environment. She constantly is thinking about what she can do to make life easier and more rewarding for her patients, for whom she displays great respect. She also is of the opinion that patients should be asked to perform certain tasks for the hospital, believing such activities would make them feel needed and recognized, whatever their contribution.

Recognition

Joelle feels that she is being constantly recognized by nursing staff, her fellow workers, and the patients she serves. She believes that we should all be thankful for what we have and that the new generation of workers for the most part displays the same commitments that more experienced staff members demonstrate at the center.

She feels that management's recognition of staff is improving and very much appreciated. She agreed that every employee should be given positive recognition regularly by their leadership team members, and staff should also recognize each other for jobs well done.

Team Building Practices and Goal Setting

Joelle agreed that staff would benefit by becoming more aware of generational profiles and how different age groups can assist and learn from each other.

This hero is very well-organized for the responsibilities she has to provide housekeeping services to a specific ward. She plans every day using a checklist model to make sure that nothing is overlooked, and her unit kept at a high level of cleanliness at all times. She uses interesting strategies for obtaining cooperation and involvement of her patients, which she feels have worked very well over the years.

The complete team meets once a month for their general staff meeting to receive the latest information from their manager. During these discussions the team determines how its members could assist their manager through group activities and "brainstorming" on how to constantly improve the quality of departmental services.

Joelle acknowledged that she and her colleagues were empowered to operate quite independently in performance of their many responsibilities – a reality appreciated by all team members, which has led to high levels of trust and support for each other.

TABOR

Tabor has worked as a transportation officer in the traffic division of one of Toronto's largest health sciences centers for the past eight years. His prime responsibility is traffic control and ensuring the safe passage of several thousand vehicles, patients and staff each day traveling to the center or dropping off patients to enter the hospital.

In addition to facilitating the extensive security and safety needs a hospital has, Tabor's duties include assisting patients in and out of wheelchairs and vehicles, frequently holding their arms and helping them safely enter the hospital. Tabor and his colleagues are also responsible for parking control, coordinated movement of public transit buses and issuing of parking tickets. The center has over one thousand beds, numerous clinics and a large long-term care facility on site.

I identified Tabor as a "Hero" after observing him over several months when visiting the hospital for medical appointments. He impressed me with his knowledge of practices and procedures, his enthusiasm, cheerful nature and willingness to do anything for anyone arriving at the center.

Tabor's enthusiasm and commitment are based on the fact that he loves people and helping everyone in any way possible. He believes that what you give to others always comes back to you in the future. He follows rules and enforces them when required to do so, and loves his work.

Recognition

The center in which Tabor works has almost 10,000 employees. Tabor has been honoured by being presented with "Outstanding Service Awards" for exemplary service on two occasions. These are amazing accomplishments for someone who truly operates within the lessons contained within The Golden Rule, "Do unto others as you would have them do unto you."

Many staff members are recognized extensively year round in a variety of ways by the various leadership and management teams of the hospital.

Team Building Practices/Interaction/Goal Setting

Tabor feels that the hospital, and particularly his department, is well-organized and that excellent relationships exist throughout the center. The philosophy within his department and throughout the organization is to respect every patient, client, and staff member, treat them with dignity, and do everything possible to make their visit and work as positive as possible.

The Parking and Transportation team meets every two weeks for a one hour meeting, during which time concerns can be raised and discussed, and planning considered for their resolution.

The team leader receives ideas from his colleagues, records them, and uses the input as a foundation for the regular departmental meetings. Tabor feels that he and his colleagues are involved, their inputs are welcomed and that they are able to contribute regularly to the success of the department.

Tabor suggested that educational programs involving the topics of teamwork and team building would be welcomed, and further strengthen the department in the future.

ROXANA

Roxana is a Registered Practical Nurse in a progressive community general hospital located in Haldimand County in Southern Ontario. She has been with the facility for over 6 years and previously worked for 10 years in another center as part of an inpatient medical surgical unit.

She takes great pride in knowing that she has done an excellent job, and being prepared to help others. She knows she can even make a greater contribution to those she serves in the future but is affected by time constraints.

Roxana feels strongly that most employees do have additional potential that has to be developed by their individual leaders. Her greatest source of satisfaction is watching the elderly persons she cares for progress successfully with their recovery to good health.

Roxana loves her work with the elderly, and assisting them in every way she can each day.

Recognition

Roxana feels recognized by the number of times staff and patients say she is doing a good job—handwritten notes are rare but appreciated. She feels that leadership would benefit by spending more time with staff learning the complexities of their jobs and by encouraging team members to contribute more to departmental operations. She noted that more contact between management and team members would assist in continuous team building. Roxana would welcome the opportunity of being of further assistance to her management team—and being further engaged within her service area.

Team Building Practices/Interaction/Goal Setting

Regular planning updates are delivered through taped recordings, and staff communicate regularly with each other. There is no formal mechanism for departmental planning and the team plans specific activities on a day-to-day basis.

There is no formal process for obtaining the input of team members to further strengthen departmental successes. The team has been empowered to work quite independently but would benefit from more involvement in contributing to the overall direction of the organization.

Roxana felt that the current administration has made some excellent changes to the overall operation of the hospital, and did suggest that the more frequent presence of managers dialoguing with staff on the floors, and within the departments, would further improve staff morale.

BONNIE

Bonnie is a unit coordinator/team leader in one of the world's top-ranked cancer centers in a large Ontario metropolitan center. She has been with the organization for 26 years and works in a specialized clinic.

A family member of mine visited her clinic regularly, during her recovery phase from cancer, and I had the privilege of observing Bonnie and how she related to both patients and staff. I was extremely impressed with her, her attitude and sensitivity, and how she always was happy and truly enjoyed serving the public. Bonnie is a cancer survivor herself and communicates regularly with patients dealing with the most complex cancer related issues in health care.

She loves her work and enjoys communicating with all patients. She is extremely proud of her organization and the wonderful care it provides to so many.

Recognition

Bonnie receives most of her personal recognition from patients, fellow staff and professional colleagues. She noted that more management presence to enhance communications would be welcomed in her area. Regular meetings to share ideas could contribute to even higher morale and improved communications. The fact that Bonnie is open to these changes, and participates in their development, demonstrates her commitment to leadership and constant quality improvement activities for both staff and patients.

Team Building Practices/Interaction/Goal Setting

Bonnie is an excellent planner. An itinerary or agenda is carefully detailed first thing in the morning when she arrives early for work. Her team of almost 20 persons meet once monthly for 45 minutes at which time agenda items, submitted earlier by team members, are prioritized and discussed for implementation.

Bonnie's team would be interested in opportunities that would allow more time to contribute to the operation of the unit, and she is certain that they could be valuable contributors to corporate leadership and future organizational successes.

Team Independence

This outstanding "Hero" reported that her team is empowered to operate quite independently within certain guidelines. All team members are well aware of their responsibilities and dedicated to the provision of high quality services to their patients. Equally important, team members are respectful of each other and willing to assist each other whenever needs arise.

LILY

Lily is the nurse manager of large ICU and critical care response team in a major teaching hospital in Southern Ontario. She has worked in health care for 38 years, the last 10 leading the Intensive Care Unit. Lily is responsible for 115 nursing full-time and part-time staff, and is dedicated to her patients and staff. She is a highly visible leader and would much rather be with her patients, families and staff than be in her office.

Some of the qualities that have made Lily a "Hero" include the fact that she loves mentoring and coaching new and current staff, and imparting to them the values of the department and her general enthusiasm. Her greatest love is to be able to attend meetings with patients and their families, to assist them in times of need, and to be part of one of the finest specialized services in Ontario.

Recognition

Lily mentioned that formal recognition for her position comes during bi-annual performance appraisals. These appraisals include 360-degree assessments by up to nine colleagues and associates. She enjoys a close relationship with the Clinical Director she reports to and obtains regular feedback within the open relationship they enjoy.

Departmental staff, organized into teams are recognized regularly by Lily. She meets with the teams often to address issues, learn, and encourage support of each other. Morale is very high within the department.

Team Building Practices/Approaches

The ICU, and Critical Response team meets regularly to discuss and handle departmental issues, and strategize on implementation of new practices and procedures. A Quality Improvement Department offers advice and guidance, monitoring progress and improvements of all groups in the center.

The team uses checklists and other documentation to make certain that targets are being met consistently. A Quality Council operates within the facility and forwards to the President numerous reports and recommendations for overall corporate implementation.

Lily explained that her department has a positive and congenial working relationship with the medical staff, who have also adopted a commitment to total quality care in every aspect of medicine.

The unit holds annual education days during the year that feature various speakers and provides an opportunity for all staff to come together for educational activities and future planning for the department.

There is little doubt that the many successes of this service are driven and supported by our "Hero," Lily. She is an outstanding, highly visible leader who is committed to her staff, patients and their future successes.

DARYL

Daryl has worked professionally for over 20 years in a large university teaching hospital in Eastern Ontario. As a member of the clergy and management team he has coached, counselled and led thousands of patients, staff, and members of the community. For the past six years he has worked on a major project designed to change the overall culture of the organization, in becoming a leader in patient and family centered care.

The efforts of Daryl and the 17-member Patient and Family Advisory Council, which meets for two hours each month, have been recognized extensively for their continuing successes. Many organizations, nationally and internationally, have visited the hospital to learn about developing a patient-focused operational strategy within their own facilities.

The patient-focused strategy includes all persons providing patient care and the recipients of those services — the patients themselves. It is essential to note that every clinical, professional and service area of the organization is involved in and contributes to this major initiative. Patient representatives, patients and family members all participate whenever decisions or changes impacting patient care are being discussed. The center has identified 61 patient experience advisors who provide input at all organizational levels contributing to improved patient care.

The basic philosophy is that everyone can learn about how patient care can be improved by listening to and learning from each other regardless of their position within the organization.

Recognition

Daryl feels that he receives recognition for his work from families, patients and colleagues. He loves what he does and is inspired to continue with leading successful change and excellence in patient care practices.

Team Building and Goal Setting Practices

The center has joined a major team building personal development system from the Cleveland Clinic in the United States. Over 40 staff were taught the principles of the HEART system and are providing instruction to all staff and physicians members within the organization. Numerous standards have been developed related to patient-centered care and are monitored and audited regularly throughout the complex. Daryl acknowledged that team members are empowered to try out new initiatives and are provided with regular support by their managers and leaders. It was also acknowledged that the patient and family centered care initiative in which Daryl is so involved will continue indefinitely into the future and is now part of overall corporate culture.

Chapter Two
Change is Weird – It Never Ends

The extensive career of our hero, Doris, has involved continuous changes over many years. She works within a constantly changing public health environment involving caring for new clients and their families, traveling to their homes, and guiding new employees. Doris applies most of the principles of management discussed in this book every day, and is dedicated to her work.

Anyone who reads this book will wake tomorrow morning and face some kind of change in his or her life. It could be any number of things, good or bad. Sometimes the change may be personal, perhaps a sick child, news of a disaster, or purchasing a new home. Change is also inevitable in the workplace, ranging anywhere from new policies to staff changes to salary increases.

The key point is that change will never stop. We will have to live with it until the end of our lives and whether positive or negative, we are faced with a choice. We can resist it or we can be adaptable and embrace it. Often, it is not the change itself that upsets or regulates the quality of our lives. That is decided more by how we handle the change. It is up to us to decide whether the change is positive or negative. If the change is inevitable, isn't fighting it a waste of time and energy? Whatever your answer, change ultimately requires us to regulate our attitudes and behaviors.

There are several reasons for addressing the concept of change. To start with, how change affects us and the ways we can cope are relevant to our attitude. Understanding change will ensure that it does not overwhelm us or create undue stress and turbulence in our lives. Also, by understanding change and its complexities, we can adapt to it more quickly and recognize from the outset what we don't like and how we can personally influence positive change. Understanding change also gives us the ability to help our colleagues better cope with the stress change creates.

Our World of Change

Our "Heroes in the Halls" are particularly exposed to change, and must adapt to it as they carry out their day-to-day work with their patients/clients and colleagues as necessary. Think about some of the changes you have experienced this year. Write them down and discuss them with your friends. You'll be amazed at how many you've had to deal with. How do you feel about the way you handled them? Happy, angry, stressed, motivated? In this chapter, we'll discuss how to cope with and manage the stress change causes while still successfully implementing the change required.

Realties of Change & Changes in the Workplace

Many types of change can occur at work including:

- Organizational / departmental structures (mergers, reporting relationships, becoming part of a regional structure)
- Provision of services regionally
- Increasing volumes of work
- Downsizing

- Technology
- Workforce profile (maturing staff, diverse populations, generational gaps)

Types of Organizational Change

Change comes in many different forms, including large-scale fundamental changes that lead to an organization or departmental shift in strategy, direction, or orientation. We must adjust what we do through fine tuning, making adjustments or altering our procedures. These are changes that may improve performance, such as when new equipment, products and systems are installed. Changes can be initiated by the individual or the team and can often lead to improved performance and increased efficiency. All staff members can contribute to such positive actions or be led by persons with the talent to implement positive change.

Personal Change

We all deal with at least three types of change in our personal lives. These include radical, adaptive, and initiated change. Although each is unique unto itself, each also has equal potential power to change our lifestyle, our outlook, and our beliefs.

Radical Change

Radical change is defined as something imposed versus chosen. It is beyond your control. Some good examples include job loss, illnesses, health care mergers, or new government policies. They are crises that impact you mentally, physically, and emotionally and, as such, may lead to new opportunities, or awakenings.

Adaptive Change

Adaptive changes are ones we may experience daily and that we adapt to simply. Matters like traffic problems, new colleagues, technology, or new taxes and policies are excellent examples. A more extreme illustration of an adaptive change is the adjustments someone who has been injured and suffered a broken neck must make. This, of course, would initially be a radical change that would be an unbelievable shock and involve months of extensive therapy. The therapy provided by many of our "heroes" would support the individual in adjusting to the new reality of not being able to walk. After considerable time the person may be able to participate in another change process called initiated change.

Initiated Change

Initiated changes are ones we can control, like stopping smoking, losing weight, having a better attitude, or planning a trip. They are usually looked upon as successes arising from our continuous efforts. For the purpose of this book, initiated change is what we will be asking our "heroes" to introduce within their personal and professional lives to improve themselves and their work place.

Why We Resist Change

There is a natural tendency for everyone to resist change. Offhand, you, personally can probably think of 10 reasons in the next 5 minutes, and within a group setting you could identify many more.

One outstanding reason is that when change occurs we sometimes become afraid. If we don't know why there has been a change, have not been told about it in advance, and have not been involved in any way with the decision leading to change, all kinds of thoughts go through our minds. These thoughts usually come in the form of questions. Will I lose my job? How will I ever retire? How will I put my kids through school? Why do we even need this? I've always supervised 8 to10 people and the new number is 5—am I being phased out? These kinds of questions can be overwhelming and lead to great stress. As a leader, you can help staff work through the fear before it becomes an issue.

Overcoming Resistance to Change

There are certain measures you and your manager can take to reduce resistance to change. One suggestion is to include people involved in the change by letting them take part in its planning, design, and implementation. Doing so demonstrates to staff that you trust they have something valuable to contribute and that their input matters. A negative work environment or lack of trust will only hurt change efforts, and participation is critical to success. As a hero, demonstrate that you will be constantly practicing positive change by explaining why the change is beneficial.

In addition, try to anticipate rational and irrational objections and determine solutions before they arise. Learn and understand what the real concerns are and implement the change step by step to allow everyone to adjust easily.

Successful Change

To help ensure successful change within the workplace, become involved in the process of bringing about a positive outcome. Explain the need for the change and establish teams or forums for accepting feedback and answering questions. Rather than focusing on only your concerns, be open to everyone's ideas and objections and let them know their input is valuable. It is critical that you explain how the change being implemented is designed to help the individual and the department.

Remember, too, that any change will always require that you clearly state the objective of the change and the strategies you will follow to make it happen. Ask your colleagues how they would like the change to operate, their concerns, and what they anticipate the long-range benefits to be for them.

Expectations for Successful Change

Successful change is any change within our lives, departments, or organizations that must include certain outcomes, including:

- Affecting the structure or way we do something (changing routines, practices, flow of work, communications, etc.)

- Causing an impact on what we are doing now (making our work easier, improving effectiveness, improving time utilization, etc.)

- Associating success with the change

- Identifying questions in advance so those involved understand the change's purpose

- Explaining the cost savings or benefits arising from the change (better quality outcomes, improved teamwork, fewer dollars and resources spent, etc.)

Should the changes you are considering not include these factors, you should alter them before you begin or don't attempt them at all.

Assessing the Change Situation

The question you may ask now is, "How do I know what to change and how will it become operational?" The following list is one guaranteed to assist any "Hero in the Hall." It's an effective tool for your personal life but more importantly for the purposes of this book, for your career. Be sure you can answer these questions to advance within your department or organization and demonstrate your leadership.

1. Who will be affected by the change?
2. Who will offer resistance and why?
3. How much time do we have to introduce the change?
4. How important is the change?
5. How much trust do we have within our department and organization?

This brief outline illustrates the dynamics behind change. Stop for a moment now and consider recent changes you've made. Might they have been less stressful for you if these questions were asked first? Remember, this book is designed to provide a new perspective about the way organizations should be managed and how team members can change their outlooks by following certain actions.

Implementing Successful Change

There is little doubt that employees or supervisors will be successful at implementing change if they understand the principles discussed and influence their teams by taking the following actions:

- Determine who needs to know about the change.

- Establish communication networks that provide everyone information about the change and the reasons behind it.

- Review the advantages of the change as compared to the previous structure/plan with everyone involved.

- Allow time for people affected by the change to review it with fellow staff members.

- Let staff members voice their objections and concerns.

- Provide an opportunity to work out solutions together to make the change more acceptable.

Being a Hero in the Hall for Change

This chapter provided an overview of the topic of change and how it can be a successful force in your personal and professional life when you're equipped with the means to implement it correctly. The information should be shared with your colleagues so that they, too, can be a "Hero." The better everyone can cope with change, the better chance it has to be successful. Participation, understanding, and a positive attitude are critical. By understanding change you can become a more valuable resource to your supervisor and colleagues, and reduce some of the threats and concerns many employees feel about the changing world we live in, as well as in our workplace.

Change should not be feared, as it is life itself. By accepting and understanding its reality, and knowing how to cope successfully, you can live a more peaceful, controlled life.

CHAPTER HIGHLIGHTS

- Change never stops, personally or organizationally.

- Why do we resist change so much?

- Change can be implemented successfully if we have a plan-what should that plan include?

- What are the major types of changes we will face constantly in our lives, personally, departmentally and corporately?

Chapter Three
Even Heroes Get Stressed

Our hero, Lily, has been a practicing nurse for 38 years. She has successfully worked in numerous stressful situations. Her current role as Nurse Manager ICU and Critical Care Response team Coordinator, places her in one of the most stressful areas in any teaching hospital. Her dedication to her patients, families and staff members reflects her ability to work and cope successfully in a complex environment. Lily applies her abilities in a calm manner based on her extensive background and devotion to her everyday accountabilities.

Everyone gets stressed. It doesn't matter who you are, what you do, or how wealthy you are. There is always something to worry about, and that something is always important. Some people would disagree, of course. Ask any parent who has a child with a long-term illness how they feel about the stresses your relatively healthy, happy family faces. You can pretty much guarantee they will be almost offended that their worries could be considered comparable to yours. The truth is, however, that stress is relative. No one person's stress level can be evaluated against another's. The bottom line is, whatever stresses you— your boss, family disputes, illness, the death of one you love– all have great impact on your life. Bearing that in mind, a new question arises. Will your stress become what defines you? Destroys you? Or, will your stress become a vehicle to make dramatic positive change in your personal life? Difficult though it is, the choice is yours to make.

Claude Halpin

Stress and Your Body

Illness

Think about your current work setting. How many times have colleagues missed work this year? If asked, sickness is the reason most would give. This may be true, but let's take it a step further. Statistics report that 75% of illness are stress-related. Stress is the single major contributor to illness worldwide. Controlling stress in the workplace is an important key in preventing heart attacks and illnesses. Applied in the workplace, a reduction of stress leads to higher productivity for employees and more understanding supervisors. These conditions lead to improved morale, increased personal and job satisfaction, and overall happiness in life for employees.

Consider the following mental health study conducted in the United Kingdom. The results show that 1 in 5 British workers said stress made them physically ill during their careers, and unmanageable pressure caused 1 in 4 to cry while at work.[1] Further, it is worth noting that prescriptions in the UK for antidepressants saw an unprecedented rise during one recent year of economic recession. Do you think the numbers are any different in North America? In all likelihood, they could be even worse.

Yes, people in the workplace will get sick. And, yes, we will always have problems, worries and fears. It is impossible to avoid stress altogether. However, our attitudes regarding stress determine how successfully we manage both in and out of the workplace.

Reacting to Stress

This brief section is describing how each of us reacts to various stress factors. From a physical perspective, it is almost impossible to control our responses. They are built into our very DNA. To protect your physical and emotional wellbeing you must be aware of what happens to your body when stress begins.

The Central Nervous System

Our bodies do some unbelievable things when something causes us to be stressed, starting with setting off an acute response alarm. Think about a common scenario when you've been frightened. Perhaps another car nearly crashed into your vehicle, or you went to see a doctor for test results you were worried about, or you were on a plane that hit sudden turbulence at 35,000 feet. What happens in frightening scenarios like these?

First, adrenalin kicks in and races through your body. Physically this means:

- Your heart beats faster
- Your blood pressure rises rapidly
- Blood goes from the stomach and skin to the muscles of the body
- High energy fats are rushed to the bloodstream for energy
- Your body releases chemicals to make the blood clot more quickly

Next, your central nervous system commands a series of physical changes.

- Pupils in the eyes dilate
- Facial muscles tense
- Blood vessels open and the face flushes
- Breathing quickens

And with that, your body is aware and ready to take action. The basic reactions we experience are universal and designed to make us sit up and take notice. We're physically forced to make a quick decision about how we should react. It's "fight or flight" —I'm going to stay here and work this out, or, I'm going to escape the present danger to give me a better chance of survival. If we decide to stay and fight, our bodies give us more power. Our heart rate increases and our body produces internal chemicals to give us additional strength and energy. The fact is, we react today as our predecessors did when fighting a sabre toothed tiger thousands of years ago.

Warning Signs

All of us experience stress but not all of us know when it's occurring. This information may make a huge difference in the outcome of the pressure. Below are additional examples of what your body experiences when stress is overwhelming you.

Emotional Indicators

Your emotions are clear indicators that your escalated stress level is, or is becoming, a problem.

- Apathy —I'm tired and don't care if things get done at work or home.

- Anxiety —I'm tense and fear what might happen and what I can't control.

- Irritability—The smallest of annoyances set me off and I respond irrationally.

- Mental fatigue—I'm so miserable that I don't know if I have the emotional strength to face another day.

Behavioral Indicators

Our behavior and reaction to stress can improve or destroy our future successes at home and at work. If you become identified as being a complainer, a lone wolf, someone who is always grumpy and unhappy, people will avoid you. And specifically at work, as time passes you'll find yourself excluded from meetings and events on an increasing basis. If you're not liked by colleagues, your opinion is less valued and your suggestions have less merit. The result? Your professional future dims.

- Avoidance—Rather than deal with my problems I'd rather pretend they don't exist.

- Extreme responses—I'm only happy with absolute perfection at home and at work, and I expect the same from others.

- These actions could cause potentially disastrous problems— I'm so defensive and unwilling to change that I could react by doing something that puts the company, or myself at risk.

Physical Indicators

Just as our emotions do, our bodies will usually tell us that something isn't right. It's up to you to interpret the signals and start doing something about them. If not, they have the potential to literally end your life.

- Excessive worry—I'm constantly agonizing that I may have every illness known to mankind.

- Denial—I'm having health problems but refuse to have them treated. I'd rather deny my issues than deal with them, even if they kill me.

- Physical exhaustion—On a daily basis I drag through my work day, put in an appearance with my family, and go to bed. I don't have the energy for anything else.

Not having energy affects our lives in too many ways to count. For starters, your work suffers and you let down those counting on you. At home, you're not fun or happy anymore and so your family begins to drift. Your emotional absence weakens the bonds with your family, putting you all at risk. And all this because of stress.

Excessive Self Medication

You find yourself trying many different medications to feel better. Side effects kick in and perhaps you no longer sleep well. Perhaps you're too excitable and nervous. Worse, a reliance on these "fixes" can become a debilitating addiction. All of these only worsen the effects of stress. It would be inaccurate to say all medication is a mistake; however, you must guard yourself about the potential problems they can cause.

Additional Indicators

There are more indicators you must be aware of if you want to avoid excessive stress. These come more in the form of common pitfalls. Successfully avoiding them means you'll have the ability to learn coping mechanisms and continue to succeed, regardless of what you're facing.

- Losing interest in personal appearance, other people, social events etc.
- Low confidence
- Low self-worth
- Procrastination
- Short-temperedness
- Overreacting
- Bottling emotions
- Setting unrealistic goals
- Racing to finish tasks

Stress in the Workplace

The reason for providing you with these general warning signs is so you have an ability to identify your own and others' reactions to stress at work. Being reprimanded by your boss, feeling overly upset over a mistake, a disagreement with another employee—any of these events will cause your body to behave as described above. Which of these has happened to you? Are there others not listed here? Determining the answer to that question is why we're discussing stress and how to control it. It is possible to change your negative reaction and become a "stress hero." It's also why you, a valued staff member, must understand what is happening with your colleagues. When you understand how stress and pressure affect you, you'll be better prepared to help others.

Work Related Stress

We should all realize that work stress is particularly destructive. The reason indicated in several studies is the fact that employees often feel powerless or don't have any control over their jobs. Worse, this is true even years after the employee has retired. The lack of control presents in later life through cardiovascular issues, depression, and many other illnesses. Job stress also shows up in hypertension and gastrointestinal disease.

In a recent study in Finland, researchers followed 5,000 middle-aged employees for almost 30 years. Researchers found that higher job stress was directly linked with more frequent hospital stays in old age even if the worker had retired.[2]

This perspective is frightening, particularly when we all know the reality is that all of us have stress at work. This is however a silver lining. It is possible to control stress.

Next, we will discuss ways that each and every "hero" reading this book can make a positive change through leadership, communications, caring, and professional teamwork. Whether on a small departmental scale or organization-wide, the power is within us to make positive changes and create exemplary businesses.

Reducing Stress in the Workplace: First Steps

1. Recognize that you can't be all things to all people whether at work, or at home

2. Make accurate assessments of stressors at work

3. Take control of what you can, when you can

4. Say no when you're overtaxed

5. Prioritize

6. Delegate

Should your manager keep adding to your agreed-upon goals, you must negotiate the requests and reprioritize them. If not, you will be stressed out and become frantic trying to cope. It becomes an ever faster treadmill, with you working harder and harder at the expense of your family, health, and possibly your job itself. We all have choices to make in life. Those regarding stress are often the ones that determine our future happiness and success.

Managing Workplace Stress as a Team

Our organizations and departments can help manage stress to a great degree with wellness programs. These can run the gamut from small matters such as controlling the climate to greater matters like addiction. You can have programs on improving nutrition, controlling weight, and encouraging exercise. All of these serve to increase endorphins, which are the hormones that give us positive perspectives on life in general. Even at work, we can empower our people to be constant contributors to our success.

By allowing participation of all staff and encouraging team work you can start developing a new type of organization. Treat others like you want to be treated—as valued members of a larger group. Be considerate in your approach to others and dedicate yourself to helping people succeed.

Just as you will begin to evaluate yourself personally for being overstressed, it's equally important in the workplace to evaluate your team. Assess whether you are all leading a balanced life—stress drops with balance.

The universal activity that benefits everyone in every way is simple exercise—30 minutes a day, 4 or 5 times weekly. Our bodies are the finest creations ever made, and they will look after you for decades if you support them.

The hope is that hundreds of thousands of "heroes" worldwide practice many of the topics we've covered. Hopefully, this book will help you to join their ranks so that you can cope with stress and benefit your family, your department and those you serve.

CHAPTER HIGHLIGHTS

- How can stress affect you emotionally and physically-what are some of the indicators of stress?

- What are some of your stressors—list what's stressing you right now and how do you plan to deal with stress in the future?

- What can the team you work with do to reduce departmental stress?

- Name three indicators-or signs of departmental stress.

Chapter Four
Generational Changes and Realities

During her seven years as an environmental services employee with a large mental health center, our hero, Joelle has worked with a wide range of staff from most generations, from brand new employees to those with many years of experience. She has adapted successfully to most situations and relationships, due to her enthusiasm, sensitivity and willingness to work with and respect new colleagues and responsibilities. She is dedicated to the residents cared for wherever she is working, and encourages them to become engaged in appropriate activities to assist in their growth and recovery. With her broad human relations skills, and understanding of human nature, generational differences are understood, respected and help her to grow within her facility.

During the past decade more attention has been paid to the fact that we live within a society that includes varied age groupings constantly facing the realities of accelerating change. This chapter will describe our current generational structures and give practical illustrations, describing the impacts of those groups – on all of us, as grandparents, mothers, fathers, brothers, sisters, managers, executives and staff. The heroes in the halls to whom this book is dedicated must have an understanding of how they can work effectively with any generation through having an understanding of the nature and timelines of the colleagues they work with.

Claude Halpin

Your Department

As we commence this chapter please give some thought to those individuals you now work with, including your leaders, your newest staff members, and the most mature members of your team. Visualize your team—how many are approaching retirement? How many are new and just taking their first "baby steps" at work? How many remind you of your own family?

To put the generational concept into the correct context think about yourself as a 20-year-old entering the work force for the first time. What was it like? How did your boss welcome you and provide for your initial orientation to your work? Finally, how did you feel—scared, nervous, happy excited, welcomed?

You can be sure that every person joining your organization or department feels the same way, and it is precisely this commonality among people that should encourage you to understand differences between the generations. As a hero, you should be willing to commit yourself to provide and receive practical coaching and mentoring about everyone you associate with at work as members of your team.

Teaching Observations

During my experiences teaching management topics to many students in all generational groups, I discovered that there were few instances when the students had not been impacted by issues, difficulties, or misunderstandings caused by factors related to their age, experience and particular generation. Every class taught over a period of years was divided into groups of 6-10 persons who were tasked with identifying and prioritizing the issues most affecting them at the time. One of the themes repeated was that of the ages of staff and related generational issues.

Some students felt that they were not being respected due to their youth and lack of practical experiences. Some more experienced team members felt they were not being respected because they were not as skilled technologically as their younger colleagues or were out of date with some skill sets such as changing technology. In this chapter I will illustrate ways in which all generations can come together with respect and dignity, driven by effective communication and recognition of the strengths of every member of staff.

Let's now review the various generations embraced within our society and see where we fit into them.

The Multi-Generational Work Force

Traditional Generation (1922-1945)

Within your department or service, you may have colleagues in this age category. In some cases, they are continuing to lead. In others, they are just now returning to the work force. They lead many of the top rated companies, departments, or services in North America.

Characteristics

These traditionalists are the historians of your department or service. They respect authority and follow directions. This generation was proud of many of its innovators who developed the Space Program, discovered vaccines for such diseases as polio, tuberculosis, tetanus and whooping cough, and prepared society for today's technological environment.

Should you have colleagues in this age range they will show loyalty and respect for your manager/leader and organization, and adhere to rules. Typically, those of this generation are detail-oriented, often referring to the past. They tend to be consistent in their behaviors and like working within a hierarchical organization or structure. Should they be managers/directors they would probably lead in a controlling fashion. In many organizations, traditionalists are board chairs or board members of private and public organizations.

The Traditional Generation finds its peers are often retiring or leaving the work force. Their family structure is changing, leading to stress as they leave what has been the focus of their life for many years.

Traditional Generation in the Workplace

An exciting recommendation you can make to your department manager is to appoint a small team of experienced, senior staff members to meet regularly to discuss what they have most enjoyed, or have been concerned about in your department over the years. Invite them to reflect on the past and capture their ideas on what they have learned and what they would recommend for future improvements. The wisdom obtained through thousands of hours and years of work experience are lost when staff retire. Invite them to use their combined wisdom to document their thoughts on how their experiences could benefit the department in the future. This initiative would be welcomed by all staff, their families, and the community and would demonstrate appreciation to all staff for their efforts over the years.

The Baby Boomer Generation (1946-1964)

We often hear about Baby Boomers and their continuing influence on society. As you consider your departmental colleagues, chances are that several are Baby Boomers and you have already noticed many of the following factors related to them.

Characteristics

This generation is often discussed as one of traditional optimism, having had many more opportunities and achievements than the previous generation. Compared to the previous generation, more had the chance to obtain an advanced education. Post-war optimism promoted a sense of stability. There were groups who had greater travel opportunities, and which witnessed great social change occurred including the Civil Rights Movement and the Women's Movement in the 1960s and 1970s. During the Baby Boomer generation, workplaces began to change from being racially homogenous and paternalistic environments to centres of racial and gender diversity.

As employees, Boomers adapt to diverse workplaces, are goal-oriented, and generally have positive attitudes. Boomers enjoy and encourage team building, collaborative decision-making and not being told what to do. They prefer avoiding conflict and have confidence in their work. Due primarily to economic reasons, many Boomers remain working after 65.

Baby Boomers in the Workplace

If you're currently part of the workforce, you probably recognize these Boomer characteristics in some of your colleagues. As with the Traditional Generation, it is important to value what they bring to the work environment. Acknowledging their belief in independence, their informed choices, their respect of hard-earned ownership, and their dedication to community involvement sets the stage for good relations. Boomers feel they could achieve anything they are committed to.

Think about the Boomers you work with. What characteristics have you observed, and what changes might you like to make to gain support or be supportive of them? Heroes should be aware of these realities and be empathetic to work situation complexities created by some of the factors described. By promoting and developing sensitive teams that know and care about each other as individuals, any department can grow to be supportive of all staff members and encourage their continuous contributions and success.

Generation X (1965-1980)

Generation X colleagues found in the workplace today range from age 35 to 50. The X-ers have grown up in times of dramatically changing technology. During their life span, they've seen mimeograph machines be left in the dust by high-speed copiers and large adding machines transformed into handheld calculators. The huge computers developed during the Traditional Generation, often large enough to fill complete rooms, have been miniaturized to desktop size for this generation. Much history has also been made during this generation's time, including the Watergate scandal to the Iranian hostage incident to the controversial Clinton-Lewinsky debacle. Another shift in Generation X from previous generations is both parents are working outside the home. The term "latchkey kids" was coined to describe children taking care of themselves, their brothers and sisters, creating more self-reliant and independent children. The number of divorces has grown during the X-ers' time.

Characteristics

Generation X-ers generally want to feel they are contributing. They seek positive feedback from their peers and leaders for their efforts. They do not want to be overly managed, preferring instead a degree of autonomy. This autonomy fuels their appreciation for independence and makes them better able to adapt to the constant changes occurring in all aspects of their personal and corporate lives.

This generation also strives for balance between their personal and family lives. They enjoy the opportunity to job share and have flexible working hours and, to achieve this, are usually very productive. Most are also technically competent and continually seek opportunities to advance within their organizations. Generation X-ers are increasingly accepting of diversity and have adapted well to a world where jobs are scarce.

When you consider your Generation X colleagues, recall that many have experienced more frequent job changes or unemployment as a result of the poor economy. This has had negative effects in more ways than financial. Loneliness and addictions are casued by weak finances. It is not your responsibility to treat the individual as much as as it is to recognize realities that can be present in any department. As a hero it is up to you to offer assistance to a colleague in difficulty, or refer them for appropriate assistance.

X-ers in the Workplace

Many of these characteristics may be seen within your department. You'll note them in employees who wish to become more independent and empowered. This comes not just from a need to control, but rather to contribute to the operation and successes through personal involvement.

Generation X-ers were hit by a severe economic recession which reduced job availability. The resulting reality check that they might not be able to have the lifestyles of their parents and relatives came as a shock to most. Many have even been forced to live with their parents again until they regained employment and could support themselves. The X-ers have often referred to as the "Boomerang Generation" because of this situation.

Generation Y (1980-1994)

Your department or service area will probably have a number of employees from Generation Y. They range in age from 21 to 35 and are also called Millennials or "Echo Boomers."

Characteristics

Generation Y has grown up in an era of advanced technology. Cell phones, laptops, and technological advancements are inherent parts of their lives. They question everything and their life stories have been shaped by historical events such as the 9-11 World Trade Center terrorist attacks and Columbine School shootings. After watching their parents lose jobs as a result of downsizing and restructuring, they find extending loyalty and trust more difficult while simultaneously feeling more determined to succeed. Slogans like Nike's "Just Do It" were predominant during these years, reflecting this outlook.

Most members of this generation came from homes where they were protected, did little to care for themselves or their homes, and felt entitled to most things in life. These workers now have high expectations of being rewarded by others with minimal personal effort. It is little wonder that some of our more mature colleagues feel the Y-ers are not contributing as much as they could and feel entitled to constant recognition.

When we look at the health care field, we see changes are escalating and job insecurity is rampant. Work could in some situations be considered temporary and unreliable. Consider how many of your coworkers, or other people you know, work at two jobs to make ends meet. This reality reduces commitments to jobs and it is up to the influence of our heroes and supervisors to encourage commitment and individual efforts of Y-ers to make departments and services better for both employees and those served.

Generation Y in the Workplace

This generation likes to be recognized and listened to. More than wealth, they are driven by the desire to enjoy life. These workers want to know how they fit into the big picture and how they can contribute to change. Their organization's structure and dynamics are of interest and they prefer to be involved in its planning and success. Positions where their external activities could be impacted are rarely preferred. Generation Y-ers staff seek continual learning and will take advantage of any training made available to them. The leaders of tomorrow will largely come from this generation, one of our youngest generations in the workplace but the most technologically advanced.

By having an understanding of the strengths of all the generations and characteristics of each, we can develop departments and services that can work in harmony to create exemplary services for those we serve. Generational differences demonstrate that we're all part of a complicated mosaic of individuals whose beliefs, challenges, and desire for respect are huge motivating factors to achieve success. Rather than seeing the mosaic as a stumbling block, heroes in the halls recognize its value and utilize the differences in a way that benefits all.

Generation Z (mid 1990's to mid 2000's)

Use internet from a young age, comfortable with technology, use social media extensively for socializing. Generation Z'ers could feel unsettled due to the Great Recession of 1998.

They are usually more conservative, more money oriented, entrepreneurial and pragmatic than Millennials.

Concerned about student debt and their futures. Are the largest portion of the US population at 26%.

At work their leaders should recognize their technological talents to improve operations

CHAPTER HIGHLIGHTS

- Why is it important for you to be aware of generational differences within your department/service?

- How can you promote generational understanding within your workplace?

- How can carefully planned orientation programs, or "buddy systems" assist in promoting generational harmony, in your department, or service?

- What are the major differences between "Baby Boomers" and "Generation "X"? What could create tension between these groups?

Chapter Five
Motivation and You

During our hero Ana's 30 years in health care she has been a highly motivated employee and manager who has faith in the talents of her staff and associates. Ana is a highly visible leader who enjoys being with her employees and colleagues, and works with them directly to resolve issues and offer advice in any situation. Utilizing her excellent communication skills and general enthusiasm, Ana develops exceptionally motivated teams dedicated to high levels of quality services for all residents.

For the most part our "heroes in the halls" are motivated to be positive, perform their duties well, and care for their patients and residents in a variety of health care settings with empathy and understanding. One of the major obligations of leaders is to provide positive environments and guidance to their staffs. It is therefore important that we understand what motivation is all about, how it impacts us, and how it can change and improve our lives.

To be motivated can mean different things, but for our heroes' purposes, we'll choose the most common definition. Being motivated means you're determined to do something, to make something happen, to deal with a problem and not procrastinate, and to successfully complete tasks. These tasks are undertaken with a drive to achieve goals in the present and help strategize for successes in the future.

A very important question I read many years ago regarding motivation is, "Who motivates the motivator?" Think about it for a moment. I cannot motivate you to read, learn and change your practices by reading this book. I can make many suggestions and provide information on how to be more effective in your role. Whether you do anything with the information is up to you and your personal motivation to proceed in new directions, learn new skills, etc. The answer to the question is, of course, that "the motivator motivates the motivator." In other words, you must motivate yourself. In the end, it is up to you to change, to learn and to enjoy the success you have earned through various lessons and experiences.

Motivating Factors

Are you highly motivated right now? Why is that? What activities, conversations and experiences have created an environment for you to do something that might be outside your comfort zone or requires greater effort? It could be anything from talking to that patient, writing that report, being on time, communicating with colleagues or planning for tomorrow. Motivation is not necessarily based on the scope of the task at hand. It is based on the personal effort it takes to achieve it. If being on time is difficult for you, any change to improve the situation is a major achievement for you and cannot be compared to some other person's efforts. Whether great or small, the goal that motivation helps you achieve will reap rewards once accomplished.

Your job and your leadership team hold many of the keys to your own personal motivation. Heroes recognize this and are able to concentrate their efforts in helping employees discover what works best for them. Many of the more common motivators yielding surprising results and new ways to develop internal talent in the workplace can be found in the list below.

Common Motivators

- Recognition for accomplishments

- Respect demonstrated by others listening to ideas and possible solutions

- Participation in the future of their department or service and its achievements

- Professional advancement

- Freedom to make decisions without being micromanaged

- Regular feedback on performance

- Opportunities to personally solve problems

- Opportunities to work with teams known to be successful in problem resolution or planning

- Opportunities to lead problem solving teams

- Trust that leaders will be transparent with their employees

- Increased flexibility in our work schedules

- Fair compensation for our efforts

Maslow's Hierarchy of Needs

Andrew Maslow's theories are important to every reader and employee of any organization. A brief overview of his premises about the needs we all have will enable you to better understand yourself, your colleagues and your leaders. When any of the basic needs described are not met, negative consequences will occur. Bearing that in mind, it's clear why understanding Maslow will enable you to react and anticipate problems based on such issues as team disharmony, organizational budgetary issues, organizational conflicts and low trust levels.

Andrew Maslow was born in 1908. He studied psychology at several universities. While at the University of Wisconsin in 1943, he published a paper entitled "A Theory of Human Motivation." It explained the concept that each person has a hierarchy of needs that must be satisfied, including physiological, safety, belongingness, love, esteem and self-actualization.

The following explanations will detail, and explain, each of the needs and how they can affect you and your colleagues.

Needs We All Share

Physiological Needs
- Food
- Clothing
- Shelter
- Survival instincts

Safety
- Protection of what we have
- Employment

Social
- Employment
- Companionship

- Acceptance
- Friendship
- Love

Esteem
- Being appreciated
- Respect
- Positive self-worth
- Praise and positive feedback

Realization or Self-Actualization

To satisfy all the basic needs listed above we have achieved the full use of our talents and potential. People who reach this level appear to be doing the best they are capable of doing.

Truly Amazing!

When we consider the talents, abilities, and potential of ourselves and those we work with we can see that there is so much we can do together to become successful individuals, and strong departments and organizations. We and our colleagues are truly amazing! The following individuals and agencies give an indication of how much we can do with what we have.

"Individuals use 10% of their potential."
- Abraham Maslow, Psychologist

"I've learned from men whom I've never met that the only real limitations I shall ever encounter are those I place on myself."[3]
- Paul Meyer, Former President of the
Success Motivation Institute

"The ultimate creative capacity of the brain may be,
for all practical purposes, infinite."
- UCLA Space Biology Laboratory of the
Brain Research Institute

These statements are a few of the many behind the development of this book. They assure us that we are capable of many things beyond what we are doing today. The power behind working together as teams, and brainstorming on future planning and resolution of issues, provide opportunities to improve what we do individually in caring and servicing others.

We recognize that those nearest the work, or activity, will always know more about that task than anyone else. For example, the housekeeper cleaning a patient's room knows more about how to do the actual process than a manager who may tour infrequently; the pharmacist who actually fills prescriptions and dispenses medications knows more about the composition of drugs and their effects on patients than most nurses who deliver the prescriptions to individual patients. Why not use their experience and knowledge to develop special projects, or "Multidisciplinary Issue Teams", to assist and provide inputs in such areas as departmental, strategic and operational planning, identifying ways to improve morale and staff satisfaction? Development of goals and objectives at all organizational levels could be considered by the same teams. This concept would also be applied to every staff member who would develop their own personal goals and manage them individually during the year.

A factor that contributes considerably to morale, engagement, and employee satisfaction is the continuous attainment of predetermined goals and objectives by everyone on staff.

By tapping the huge potential of our staff we can become much stronger and provide increased support to our organization, at all levels, while empowering employees to become more involved in their own organizational lives.

The time has come to encourage and promote an environment of participation for every staff member, allowing them to contribute directly to the ultimate success of any department or service.

Destroying Motivation

There is a flip side of positive and productive motivation. Sometimes organizations and individuals can de-motivate and demoralize teams through a variety of practices including:

- Threats
- Penalties
- Unconstructive criticism
- Demotions
- Reduction of benefits
- Changes without consultation
- Dictatorship
- Need for constant approval
- Micromanaging
- Poor support, guidance, and training
- Negative language

Use of these practices will guarantee higher absenteeism, low levels of trust and minimal production. Staff must be – deserve to be! – treated with dignity, respect and involvement in order to have their basic needs fulfilled. This fulfillment will go a long way to ensuring their loyalty to their departments and organization.

Strengthening Motivation

Motivation is the inner desire or power that drives you to achieve something specific. You might want to lose weight, learn a new language, buy a new car, or become the best department or service in your organization. Once you have determined where you want to go, motivation will get you there with enthusiasm and excitement. Without any targets or goals you will not be motivated to achieve major tasks, and life will go on as it did last week, last month and last year.

Motivation is present when you have defined a clear vision for yourself, know precisely what you want to do, have specific goals and a desire to proceed with full confidence in your abilities. Motivated people take action and do what is necessary to achieve their goals, and are happier and more productive. They are motivated to visualize success and can see the success on that large screen TV in their minds.

More on Strengthening Your Personal Motivation

- Set goals: Write them down and break them into smaller minor goals you can successfully work on until the major task is finished. This approach will increase your motivation to do something and not be overwhelmed by some huge task.

- Finish what you start: Always close the loop on any activity. You'll feel better knowing a task is completed.

- Don't procrastinate: Procrastination leads to laziness, which leads to a lack of motivation.

- Be persistent and persevere: Keep yourself motivated at all times in spite of any difficulties or problems that may arise.

- Visualize: See yourself as being successful through a positive attitude and high level of motivation. You should be able to see yourself completing projects, achieving targets, and being rewarded for your efforts in many ways.

Auditing Motivation

As heroes in the halls and leaders we should always be aware or have a means of determining how well our team is being motivated. If you are a manager or supervisor it is important to be highly visible and in contact regularly with your colleagues. Regular and confidential staff surveys will take the pulse of the team, identify the level of motivation within the team and take corrective action as necessary to raise motivational levels.

A highly motivated team can accomplish amazing results and create a workplace where people are happy and love their jobs. Motivation comes from within the individual. We must listen to each other and recognize the fact that we are living in environments of constant change. Together, we can create structures that challenge us, motivate us, and allow us to contribute to our future successes.

CHAPTER HIGHLIGHTS

- What does the word "motivation" mean to you?

- List the factors which motivate you?

- What lessons and practices can you learn from "Maslow's Hierarchy of Needs" and why is it so important for us to understand them?

- List activities that can destroy, or encourage, motivation.

Chapter Six
Visioning: Let's See About That

Our hero, Catherene, has practiced for over 20 years as a professional nurse in two community general hospitals. Her most recent position in Eastern Ontario has been in a process of change and expansion for several years. She has been a participant in many successful change endeavors and visioning experiences as the organization has gone through major redevelopment to design its future. She has adapted and leads a new concept of management, which encourages constant organizational improvement. It is called the "LEAN" System. "The system involves daily departmental inputs or "huddles" where all staff identify issues and strategies for their resolution" . LEAN is also a forum for general teambuilding and dialogue at all organizational levels.

If I say the words "North Pole" we all instantly visualize what it looks like. That image is created by our perceptions, past experiences, pictures, and stories. This is true in the workplace, too. Our routines build into us the ability to "see" the task at hand. The kind of business is immaterial. For instance, a corner grocer may envision restocking shelves. A pharmacist may envision filling prescriptions. Alternately, employees will envision what they've yet to experience, too. An employee at an IT company may think of what it will look like to install a new system, including not just the process but the reactions of fellow staff and potential obstacles.

At this point you're probably wondering what any of this has to do with Heroes in the Halls. The answer to that question is not simple. Many perspectives come into play in understanding exactly why visioning is relevant in this case; however, know this: visioning is one of the most important concepts we will ever learn personally, departmentally, and corporately.

I'll now ask you to close your eyes and picture a blank 60 inch flat screen television. You will see it instantly—you can't help not seeing it. For the purposes of this chapter, we'll consider it a canvas you can use to paint your visions.

Defining Visioning

A broad definition of visioning is using imagery within ourselves to paint vivid pictures. You have the ability to visualize anything. Just thinking of that new car you want to buy, how your new home should be decorated, or an upcoming vacation will bring instant images to mind. As soon as you think about anything the picture of it will pop up on that 60 inch screen.

Visioning as a Planning Tool

Personally

Visioning can be used on a personal level as well as a departmental one. For a moment, set aside your yearly goals. What do you want your personal life to look like in five years? Visualize that on your screen. Do you look the same? Are you happy about that? How is your lifestyle different? Have your relationships changed? When considered on a personal level, visioning can help you set reasonable goals and, moreover, gives you an opportunity to plan. What do you need to do to achieve your goals? The alternative is not something to look forward to, as it usually presents as a person waking up and realizing that nothing much has changed, or that nothing has changed for the better.

Professionally

Let's now move on to the world of work. It's really not all that different from visioning your personal life. Are you the leader of your department now or are you lower on the corporate level? Do you want that to change? Or, perhaps you're already quite successful and have become bored. Is it time to become an entrepreneur? Switch fields altogether? The point is that you can do any of these if you continue to picture them on that 60 inch screen. Set near-sighted goals that will enable you to meet the far-sighted ones, and plan accordingly. It will come to fruition because you, a hero, know exactly what you want. Failures and problems will not inhibit your success because you can see where you want to be at the end of the journey.

Organizationally

You can create a vision for your organization, too. Is there any reason why the department you work in or the service you offer is not the top performer in its area? Any reason why it doesn't reflect the highest quality standards, lowest turnover, and highest staff satisfaction levels? Imagine you can think of many reasons why not, instead of just one. Not enough money, lack of trust, excessive work loads, poor management, etc. are all valid concerns that inhibit success. However, the power of visioning can transform situations like this. Allowing a department or organization to use visioning as a team instead of asking them to do it individually brings everyone together. Open discussions follow and common goals are set. Even negative matters, like dissatisfaction on the part of employees or a sense of disrespect perceived by the employers can be addressed in a non-threatening manner. In this setting, visioning begins with a clean screen that the team develops together. Where they want to go, what their goals will be, and the many benefits associated with major improvements they will spearhead are clear and possible for all.

Implementing a Vision

Early in my career I had the privilege of being selected to lead a specialized 2,500-bed facility for people with disabilities, and a staff of 1,800 members. The center was a place of chaos—overcrowding, low funds, exceptionally high turnover, little pride and little trust. And yet, with all of these issues, there were still hundreds of "heroes in the hall" who provided the best services they could with what resources they had.

The challenge for our team was to restore a sense of calm, service excellence and pride within the organization. After several meetings with the leadership team we agreed to reach for the stars and aim for achieving something never accomplished before. We wanted to be the first health care organization to gain accreditation, the highest recognition and gold standard for health care facilities in Canada.

Our senior leaders and all department managers carried this message to every employee and asked for their help and involvement to achieve this seemingly impossible goal. Without them, it literally wasn't possible. We placed positive posters throughout the center every month that depicted some aspect of accreditation, like teamwork, caring and listening. We worked with the local newspaper to tell our story and held countless productive meetings with our teams. After two years of effort, we met our goal. We were the first special facility of this kind in Canada to gain Provisional Accreditation status. This is a superb illustration of how having a vision and pursuing it with passion and commitment as a team can produce outstanding results that benefit all. Together, we visualized the plan for where we wanted to go, what we wanted to become, and how we intended to get there. This concept can apply to any department or service. You can make wonderful things happen personally or departmentally if you can see them on that large TV screen.

The Pictures Vision Create

Visions have the power to do many things for the heroes reading this book:

- They engage our imaginations and show powerful images of the outcomes we want.

- They allow others to see where they or their organization is going.

- They help guide and plan future actions.

- They help us focus on specifics, not generalities.

- They challenge us to set new practices and levels of performance.

Visioning helps heroes in more ways than what you'll find on this list. Coping with pressure and stress, resolving problems, and promoting a lifetime of success are all results of visioning. Below are a few illustrations of "visioning in action" and how it came to the rescue and ensured success.

Claude Halpin

A Hero in a Conflict Situation

Suppose your manager asks you to meet to discuss concerns he/she has about your recent performance. He's never expressed dissatisfaction with your work and so this request comes as a shock to you. Immediately, your thoughts are clouded with doubt about your performance and what you possibly could have done wrong. The situation is made even murkier considering that you don't know him well outside an impression that he treats his employees fairly and is an excellent planner. Rather than letting his thoughts move in a negative direction, this is the moment a hero has to visualize a positive outcome. The first thing to do is try to set aside the concern for a time. If nothing can be done to change the situation, it's smarter to put it on the back burner. When the visioning process begins later, you'll have a clearer mind.

When evening comes and you've settled in at home, allow yourself to see the screen before you. Rather than trying to see what you do not know with negative images, use this opportunity to let your 60 inch flat screen TV come to life with the pictures of the strong performance you know you've had. Next, imagine what the picture could look like after you meet with your manager. Be open to his ideas and know that you can incorporate them in your personal TV screen.

Don't stop with visioning the positive. Live in the moment and, rather than letting the matter consume you, begin to visualize yourself having a peaceful sleep and awakening refreshed and positive. Set yourself up for success.

Constantly see yourself on your personal internal TV screen and allow your visions to calm you, guide your activities and accomplish every goal you have planned for the future.

CHAPTER HIGHLIGHTS

- What does the word 'visioning' mean to you?

- How can you use visioning, both at work, and within your personal life?

- Why is it important for you to "see" something, on that 60 inch screen, in your brain", before you do anything?

- What are some of the benefits of using visioning in your life both personally and at work?

Chapter Seven
Goals and Objectives for Success

Our hero, Bonnie, has served in a large teaching hospital for 25 years. She currently is a Unit Coordinator/Team Leader of a specialized service. Through good planning, problem resolution and excellent communication skills Bonnie contributes to an exemplary team. Her department cares for complex patients who may attend her service for many months during their recovery periods. She leads through careful planning and team achievement of pre-determined goals, all designed to maintain the highest quality of care to all patients. Bonnie is enthusiastic, caring and dedicated to those she and her team serve.

The foundation of any successful endeavour is based on the consistent completion of pre-determined goals. This is true regardless of whether the endeavour is personal or professional. Without goals we drift aimlessly, doing the same things over and over, and become too comfortable in our careers and lifestyles. Work becomes stagnant and we're locked into a repetitive cycle of sameness. Better put, we quit striving to become better.

This doesn't have to be the case, however. Our futures can be exciting and our organizations can be exemplary, regardless of their current status. There's no time limit on taking charge and making change. This is something essential for our heroes to understand. Setting goals, designing actionable steps, and taking initiative is all you need to change your course from stagnant sameness to motivated advancement.

Successful Goal Setting

Let's return to the analogy used in our last chapter. In some ways, goal-setting is quite similar to visioning. In this case, you can set goals by imagining scenes unfolding that show where you want to go (goals) and how you're going to get there (actionable steps). In addition to being great visioning tools, goals represent the commitment that you're determined to change and grow. They also determine the actionable steps you will take to move from one place to another based on your vision of the future.

It's imperative to have short-term and long-term professional goals combined with short-term and long-term personal goals. Having both will guide you along the path you have carefully crafted and will keep you focused instead of simply drifting along with your life or career.

Finally, goals must specifically identify what will be achieved and the results the achievement will yield. They also must be measurable and there must be an exact date identified for taking measure.

The Process

People are often leery of setting goals, believing the process will be overwhelming or present what they can't live up to. This is absolutely untrue. Achievements and successes can and will happen, and everyone has the ability to plan for the next few years if they use the following basic method.

1. List all the goals you would like to achieve in the future, and identify whether they're personal or professional goals (I want to lose 20 pounds in the next 10 months vs. I want to complete two courses towards a college diploma by next September).

2. Review the list and prioritize each item based on its importance to you.

3. Carefully develop plans for the three top items and then use specific criteria to measure and achieve them.

4. After you have met the first three goals, revisit your prioritized list and identify the next three targets.

5. Repeat this process until you have completed all of your prioritized items.

The key to success with this method is that you aren't taking all of the goals on at one time. You recognize them, that's true, but you've broken them down into smaller, doable achievements. Not doing so is a common mistake made in goal-setting. People who begin the process motivated and excited to make a change can end up discouraged, defeated, and right back where they started. They're back to the status quo and less likely than ever to move ahead.

Just the facts and nothing but the facts!

Imagine yourself building a house. Does it just happen? Do truckloads of lumber and supplies simply materialize? Is there a vague idea that becomes an obvious plan just by taking a hammer in hand? Of course not. The process begins with obtaining hundreds of facts and a visualization of your new home. Blueprints, deadlines, and contractors must be made and chosen. There must be a detailed construction "symphony" before you even begin blueprints, much less construction.

We know we can achieve so much and so can our colleagues, teams and organizations, once we know where we're going. Based on managerial studies we also know that for every minute or hour spent planning, we will be given a return on our investment ten times over. That's why setting goals and objectives allows us to achieve so much. Goals should be uniquely your own and not a rehashing or copy of something belonging to someone else.

Professionally speaking, goals should be pursued with the whole team involved and an examination of what the current reality is. As a group, you must agree on a plan regarding advancing into the future. Consider it time to turn on the station on the TV set you've visualized.

The Six Essential Questions

Who, what, when, where, why, and how? These six questions can assist you and your team immensely in achieving successful goals. Not many ask them because, although seemingly basic, they're scary. However, if you do ask these questions in goal-setting activities with your team, you will be provided with practical answers to your planning questions.

Who?

When we ask 'Who?' we don't necessarily mean who the new goals and plans will affect. They will affect everyone. Such is the ripple effect of change. In asking 'Who?' what we really mean is, "Who will be the leader in accomplishing this goal? Who will be the hero?"

What?

We've already established that deciding goals and actionable steps is accomplished by knowing predetermined targets and objectives, which we develop individually or in group settings. These targets help us to assess situations and prevent costly errors. So, the question of 'What?" is not just about the plans themselves. It's about what's needed to make them happen, and what's needed is a hero with confidence.

When?

A confident hero builds performance standards into existing plans and monitors performance regularly. Heroes know the standards and monitoring process and know that at any time they can make adjustments quickly with minimal disruption to the team's activities. The question of when to assess goals is, really, any time it seems needed.

Where?

The answer is easy. Anywhere. It doesn't matter the organization or your place in it. Successful heroes who are ready to lead change and accomplish goals can be found at every level.

Why?

We've already established the reason for goals, and with this essential question we're once again back to heroes. Why we need heroes is simple. Without heroes leading the way, it isn't possible for a team to advance. Rather than wondering why a hero is needed, ask yourself instead, are you ready to be that hero?

How?

How workers establish themselves as heroes is through action, experience, and leadership. It is your reaction to goal-setting, your level of involvement, and your initiative that will determine how people see you as a hero in this sense.

Personal Planning

We all know that time goes by very quickly. To keep on top of our future aspirations we should take time two or three times a year just to consider our lives. It's important to assess what we have and have not achieved and identify what success means to us on a regular basis.

One oft-posed question is whether we're happy with what we're earning. If not, what strategies are available to achieve new goals and targets?

I recently spoke with a human resources specialist who decided she wanted to work independently, set her own deadlines, and hire others to help her. In just two years she was doing exactly that. She was earning as much as ever, controlling her own time, and delivering exclusive quality services to clients she prefers to work with. It sounds far-fetched but the opposite is true.

She brought about these changes by setting firm goals and staying on track, something all heroes are capable of. You can change your life and improve its quality once you understand that everything is driven by planning. Look at yourself in the mirror every day and remind yourself where you want to go and, most importantly, know that you can do it!

The SWOT Analysis: The Secret of Great Planning

SWOT is an acronym for Strengths, Weaknesses, Opportunities and Threats. A consideration of each will provide you with a complete overview of where you, your department, or your organization stands at any time within these operational areas. This simple analysis is one I have used to complete numerous organizational and departmental strategic and operational plans and never has it failed to produce remarkable results. A SWOT analysis is equally effective in setting personal goals and objectives and is conducted in much the same way.

Strengths:

List all of your personal strengths. Are you a people person? Do you complete tasks on time? Are you detail-oriented? Be sure the list is comprehensive—the strengths are your greatest tools in achieving your goals. It's a good idea to run this list by someone, too. Sometimes people have strengths they don't even realize.

Weaknesses:

Make a list of the areas in which you don't shine, and be honest about it. The bottom line is that we all have weaknesses. It doesn't help us to pretend otherwise. In fact, to do so practically guarantees goals won't be met. Perhaps you're not a good planner or aren't assertive enough, or perhaps you tend to be controlling or stubborn. If these are true, own it and consider it room for growth. And, like strengths, it's not a bad idea to ask someone else for an opinion. Be aware that in this case it won't be so rewarding.

Opportunities:

Identify what you see as possibilities for growth in your future. Maybe you envision having a position in a new local hospital, teaching part-time at a college, or working towards a college diploma or university degree. It doesn't matter how big or small the possibility is. Simple or extreme, all opportunities that change your life in any way are of equal importance.

Threats:

Finally, list everything you consider as threats to your success. If you lack a trait considered important in achieving your long-term goal, you should identify it early on so you have time to improve or change. Examples of such threats would be a lack of communication skills or strong credentials. Other threats may be more personal. Are there facets of your life that will get in the way of achieving your goals easily, such as family demands on your time? All of these can be adjusted if you acknowledge them now and commit to changing them.

By completing this initial diagnostic you will have taken a major step to future success. With it, you now have the ability to create a plan that addresses significant matters assisting with or impeding your success. Remember that it would be impossible to work on all the topics you've listed at one time. Prioritize each of the lists and choose only one or two from each to begin. Don't let the length of the list discourage you. By conducting the SWOT analysis you've already taken strides you should feel proud of.

Other Critical Factors

Those of us in the business world know that over 50% of all strategic or operational plans fail because of repeated specific practices. The same percentage may apply to personal plans as well. Chief among these practices is failure to develop complete action plans that address each prioritized issue you've recognized. Below you'll find more instructions that will teach you, step by step, how to create a successful plan to achieve your goals.

Action Plan Instruction Kit

1. Name the prioritized issue you are considering changing or improving.

2. Carefully consider then itemize what actions or strategies are required to completely resolve or correct the issue.

3. Identify who will be responsible to provide the leadership for a successful conclusion. In personal circumstances, that person is obviously you. This is not necessarily true in a professional arena. A hero with the ability to create successful action plans can recognize who the best leader is to correct different problems faced.

4. Know what resources are required. Do you need a change in time, technology, finances, work space, etc.?

5. Set a start date for project.

6. Determine an estimated date of completion.

7. Know how the plan will be monitored for success while being implemented.

8. Identify how you will determine when the stated goal has been met.

By developing a basic form with these items you will ensure that everything you do will have a good chance of succeeding. Attention to detail and a proven planning strategy are critical.

Departmental or Organization SWOT Analysis

Whether the process you're undertaking is personal or job related, the principles are the same. Workwise, however, they include more teamwork and a healthy respect of each team member's thoughts.

1. Analyzing strengths, weaknesses, opportunities, and threats with team analysis and brainstorming

2. Identifying the most important issues under each heading

3. Appointing individuals who will be responsible for each of the prioritized issues

4. Requiring appointed individuals to prepare action plans for each item to address and fixing accountabilities accordingly

5. Identifying dates for completion of tasks

6. Monitoring progress through regular feedback

7. Implementing the plan

8. Revisiting and reprioritizing goals as the initial ones are met. The cycle of planning should be repeated each year, whether individually, departmentally, or corporately

Planning is a critical part of the lives of all of our "Heroes in the Halls" across Canada and North America. This chapter has been designed to assist them personally and corporately with effective planning activities. A commitment to consistent planning will ensure their future successes as leaders providing caring, organized, and successful services to the tens of thousands of patients, residents, and clients they look after every day of the year.

CHAPTER HIGHLIGHTS

* Why is it so important to have written goals both at work and personally?

* What are the six essential questions to ask when you, or your team, are setting both personal, or departmental, goals?

* What is a "SWOT" analysis, and why is it one of the most powerful tools ever for both personal, and departmental planning?

* Have you written personal goals for next year? Why are you waiting?

Chapter Eight
Teamwork – Personal and Group Success

For the past eight years our hero, Tabor, has worked as a member of a 37 person parking and transportation services team at a large teaching hospital. He has been recognized two times by being awarded an "Outstanding Service Award" by the leadership of this 10,000 employee organization. His successes, along with those of his colleagues, could never have been achieved without his being part of a department that encourages and expects exceptional teamwork every day of the year. Tabor is an outstanding team player and is passionate about doing his very best, every day, to treat everyone he meets with respect and making their visit to his hospital as pleasant as possible.

Everyone reading this book, whether a hero already or someone aspiring to be a hero, is a member of some kind of team. By definition, teams include members who work together to achieve a common goal. That's too simplistic for our purposes, however. In this book, teamwork is not just working toward a common goal. It's working toward that goal with respect, with openness to ideas, effort, service and communication. Effective teams are necessary to guarantee the success of any organization or department. Pay attention, and you'll see that successful teams are led by caring leaders who are sensitive to individual needs and are visible frequently within the department or organization. Successful teams are led by heroes.

Features of Exemplary Teams

Based on many years of experience in leading health care facilities and working with numerous executives, directors, managers and general staff, I've learned that exemplary teams have specific, invaluable skills and traits that are fundamental to their success. These traits include:

- Mutual respect between teammates and leaders
- A willingness to step in to help each other
- A sharing of corporate wisdom and experience
- Regular praise and recognition
- Leaders who maintain a presence in the team's work area
- Opportunities to share visions for departmental growth and change
- Goal-setting exercises
- Shared knowledge of annual targets for their department
- Opportunities to learn about activities and systems beyond the team's department
- Strategic goals and objectives development
- Mutual agreement regarding roles to play
- Educational opportunities for personal development and, ultimately, departmental success
- Fun and friendly atmospheres

Building Team Trust and Understanding

Team members should encourage departmental trust. One way to do this is to openly discuss ways in which trust can be maintained. This is not something achieved overnight, but rather a process of time and evidence.

One of the most effective ways of developing trust is to involve the team. Ask them to define and develop their understanding of what trust means to them. This starts with bringing the team together and dividing into small groups of 4-6 people each.

Teammates are asked to explain to their group what trust means to them. The responses are noted and discussed within the group and the participants are asked to rank the definitions. The most frequently mentioned definitions are recorded on flip charts for discussion. This approach is followed for each group and when all definitions have been recorded the combined group ranks the definitions by priority from 1 to 3. After these priority items are discussed as a complete group, a final trust statement is developed as an operating commitment for the full team to follow in the future.

When the whole team is involved in establishing what trust means, they are more invested in its success. Your team has the answer. As a hero, it is your job to listen to them, let the answer be developed, and help implement it.

As mentioned earlier, generational profiles and differences can sometimes impede trust until the parties have worked together and have gotten to know one another. An example of a trust problem would be having a 60-year-old food service worker placed with a 24-year-old colleague before they have the opportunity to become acquainted through an appropriate orientation process. Unless such orientation occurs, generational conflicts and misunderstandings can occur, which could be negative for the individuals and the team as a whole.

Building positive relationships and effective teams starts on Day One and should be standard practice across the organization. One way to accomplish this is by using a "buddy" system. In this system, a mature and experienced worker is assigned the job of educating a new employee on departmental operations and organization. The system applies to every part of the organization, whether for the Board of Directors, managers, or lower level employees. Regardless of administrative level, all new colleagues need advice and coaching from experienced team members.

Problem Solving and Team Building Activities

The power of group activities within teams cannot be over-emphasized. After working with hundreds of groups I have rarely encountered one that could not identify solutions to any issue presented to them within a short period of time. Teams are waiting to help leadership—they simply have to be given the opportunity to do so.

Should the manager of any team involve his staff in identifying issues and developing operating plans through group brainstorming activities, there is no reason not to let the team itself come up with solutions for any of the areas of concern. Several staff members can also be taught to facilitate such group processes and present solutions to the leader after working with team members. There are few areas of departmental operations that cannot be resolved through this type of activity. Be the hero of your team and try it—it will work.

Another way to ensure that teams will succeed is by using others as a comparison or guide.

It's smart to visit, and observe, other departments in action. By observing other successful teams, they will see positive examples they can apply themselves. Sometimes, they will observe the opposite: teams who aren't functioning well together. This, too, provides an excellent example in its own way. It's often easier to spot someone else's mistakes than your own. Once a team sees how the same mistake is affecting them, changes can be made.

A working example of this would be to have housekeeping staff visit nursing wards with the supervisor or manager. The nursing supervisor would brief them on the functions of the area, and their day-to-day challenges. This activity will lead to improved understanding and lessons learned which improve teamwork, including teamwork between the departments.

Becoming an Effective Team Player

We have discussed many ways for you to become an effective team player including:

- Doing your best as a team member
- Supporting your leader and letting he or she lead
- Being flexible and willing to compromise or change
- Going beyond your own job responsibilities for the benefit of your team
- Sharing your experiences with other team members
- Assisting with resolution of issues
- Being willing to become a "buddy", or mentor, to new colleagues
- Making an effort to get to know the strengths, of as many of your colleagues as possible
- Working collaboratively with other staff members to get things done

Members of strong, effective teams are committed to looking beyond their own work assignments and contributing as necessary to overall departmental success.

Teams consist of a wide range of individuals, all having certain strengths and limitations. If you compare your current work team to a hockey, football, basketball, or baseball team you observe that every team has players who do different things because they are the best at that given skill. Everyone cannot be the quarterback or goalie, but they might make an excellent lineman, kicker, runner, or receiver. Recognizing differences is critical to reaching an understanding of why colleagues must be treated with respect. Employees deserve to be acknowledged and valued for the expertise they've gained during their career.

Many of our heroes belong to exceptional teams that excel in what they do. These are teams who know that they can be the very best through participation, respect, planning and visioning.

CHAPTER HIGHLIGHTS

• What are the characteristics of a good team player, and are you one?

• List five factors which contribute to successful workplace teams.

• What does "trust" mean to you and how can it be developed personally, and within your department, or organization?

• How can groups of staff be used most effectively in problem resolution activities and planning activities?

Chapter Nine
Communication

Our hero, Daryl, is a member of the clergy and a senior executive team member of a major teaching hospital in Eastern Ontario. He has held these positions for over 20 years. In his current role he has been deeply involved with a project dedicated to patient and family centered care. This role requires exceptional communication and listening skills as it involves numbers of patients, their families and all levels of staff, dedicated to a commitment to have patients being considered as "partners" within the complex. Daryl enjoys the excitement of learning from others, particularly patients, and the challenge of having them become integral contributors to increasing levels of care, understanding, and communications at all organizational levels.

Communicating well is one of the greatest skills heroes can develop. Research has determined that every day we spend 70% to 80% of our time communicating in one way or another. In light of that reality, it naturally follows that effective communication skills will have a great bearing on the successes in our lives.

Knowing the basic principles of effectively communicating and listening is critical to success. To begin, note that effective communication includes speaking, writing and listening. And, while it's true that this is the lifeblood of a workplace, good communication stretches well beyond that.

Our communication and interactions with our families, friends, and people within general society is critical. Communication skills were also learned from leaders in our lives who were, and are, excellent communicators including: Winston Churchill, John F. Kennedy and President Obama. People known throughout history as famed communicators add to our understanding of this concept as well. Skills commonly used by strong communicators are below. Think of the people in your lives that you've admired (or *didn't* admire) in history that demonstrate these:

- Knowing the message
- Making certain the message was received
- Listening for responses
- Questioning feedback to make sure the message was clearly understood
- Replying to feedback and following up
- Staying focused while communicating
- Making eye contact while speaking and listening
- Demonstrating an openness to dialogue
- Speaking clearly
- Keeping an open mind to avoid conflict
- Being aware of an audience's ability to comprehend the message

Defining Communication

Communication involves the transmission and understanding of information from one person to another through the common methods described below. To be sure that we're getting the right message, to the right source, at the right time as understandably and efficiently as possible, it's important to keep our communications well-structured. As a staff member you will be judged by your supervisors and colleagues on how well you communicate and the more effective you are, the better your opportunities to advance and become a leader. Effective communication is also key to our successful work with patients, the public and other agencies.

The Written Word:

Whether in the form of letters, reports, instructions, minutes or plans, the written word is the basis of most corporate and departmental communication. It is relatively permanent and easily accessed. With such predominance it stands to reason that reading and writing effectively are imperative to success.

The Spoken Word:

Speaking and listening are the backbone of this form of communication. Conversations, meetings, interviews, phone conversations, and general announcements are the way most organizations communicate immediate news and instructions daily. These also open dialogue between individuals and departments. If managed well, the spoken word can be a powerful tool; however, if mismanaged, the spoken word can cause strife and confusion.

Gestures and Body Language:

Gestures and body language, both conscious and unconscious, affect people greatly. They include both positive and negative behaviors you demonstrate for an intended target.

Examples of negative behaviors are rolling or closing your eyes, crossing your arms or making no eye contact. Additional examples are tone of voice and facial expressions. Think about your work day and ask yourself, what messages am I conveying as I interact with others?

Visual Images and Presentations:

Visual images are used to convey conscious and unconscious messages to various target groups within an organization, and include photographs, models, charts, DVDs, illustrations, etc. Once these visual images are in our minds, their power is difficult to reverse. Take caution and proceed carefully before you present something that will have this great impact. The benefit of a visual image's power is important to remember, too. The better your presentation, the more favourably memorable it will be.

Multimedia:

All media is impactful whenever it can be used extensively to communicate consistent information to viewers and listeners. Media combine the different methods of communications and extensive use of information technology. Examples include television, newspapers, company publications and social media sites. More and more we see social media being used to sway public opinion. We're also discovering that what you publish or profess online can never truly be erased. Be aware of that when you give bold statements or opinions.

Barriers to Communication

As mentioned earlier, communication is the lifeblood of any organization. Therefore, it is important to identify certain factors which lead to communication difficulties. Consider situations you have encountered where communications were problematic. What made the situation a problem and how did you adjust to it? Chances are some of your communication problems could have been a result of any of the following factors:

Improper Timing

An example of improper timing would be if you were working under pressure to complete a project and your supervisor gave you another major new assignment without additional resources or support. You become stressed, view the project negatively, don't ask appropriate questions and proceed with your daily work simply assuming you will somehow get the new task completed at some time even if you don't know how or when.

Environmental Disturbances

Picture a scene where you're having an important meeting with two other colleagues and can't hear what is being said due to disruptive noise outside the meeting. Under such circumstances you may miss important words or instructions and be forced to ask that they be repeated. It's important not to move on until you have received the complete message. If you fail to do so, it's likely you'll end up redoing the task later.

Improper Behaviors

Suppose you're in a meeting with several colleagues and one starts accusing another of a negative action. The accused person storms out of the room and slams the door and the room is now silent. The group quickly realizes that the dialogue should be revisited.

Upsetting situations destroy effective communication and should be prevented if possible. If they occur, the spokesperson or leader should acknowledge the event and state that the meeting will be proceeding with the original agenda. Some leaders may take the opportunity to discuss the event, ask the team to share their perceptions of what happened, and propose specific solutions should anything similar occur in the future.

Background Differences

North America is becoming more and more diverse, creating a truly multicultural society. We provide health care and long-term care to people with backgrounds from around the world. Sometimes these differences require careful understanding to make sure that the messages sent or instructions given are totally understood by every individual, otherwise communication problems could occur.

Sender Receiver Relationships

Poor communication often occurs if there is a dislike among staff. Personal feelings prevent listening carefully, or interpreting correctly what is being said. This misinterpretation can result in major errors in performance or task completion. The leading supervisor in this situation should be the catalyst to help the involved parties work out an acceptable solution within a specific timeframe.

Listening Skills

The majority of our time is spent listening to a wide range of communications each day. This begins at home. Each morning we listen to the discussions with our family members, we listen to the radio while driving to work, or to the sounds of our fellow passengers on the bus or subway. When we reach the workplace, we converse with our colleagues as we enter our hospital or facility and, once inside, we listen to reports on activities that have occurred since we were last at our job, and hear our new assignments.

During the day, we are constantly talking with or listening to our patients, team members and colleagues from many areas of our facility. At the end of the day we go home and once again become part of our family communication network. This continues until we finally reach the end of our day, go to bed and hopefully have a peaceful sleep until we wake up and start the day's cycle of listening once again. It's a barrage of information to process.

Defining Listening

Listening is the ability of receiving and interpreting messages. It's a basic life function and key to all effective communication. What we hear and how we listen are important and very different skills to consider. Listening is the key to all effective communication. Without the ability to listen well, messages can be misunderstood, leading to a communication breakdown. The sender of the message can become frustrated or irritated and the intended recipient is confused.

Listening requires us to focus, whereas hearing refers to the sounds you hear and pay attention to. The use of language, tone of voice and body language of the person speaking tell us volumes. To be an effective listener, you must be aware of verbal and nonverbal messages. We can all be better listeners by following a few critical steps.

Pay close attention to the speaker:

What really is the message being sent and are you understanding what is being said?

Concentrate and focus on what is being said:

Ask for clarification. If you don't, eventually you will have to again ask the person you were speaking with. Asking when the information is first shared shows initiative and attentiveness. Waiting until later can make it seem as though you didn't care to during the earlier discussion.

The Irony of Poor Listening Skills... and What Speakers Can Do About It

Numerous studies have shown that we retain and understand little after hearing presentations or having conversations with team members and other staff.

Just 48 hours after listening to new information being shared, most of us only remember 25% of what was discussed.

If that's true, you can see how poor listening would lead to problems on the job, associated with missing instructions, not carrying out tasks or transmitting information. Ironically, our incredibly and capable fast brains are what cause the problem of not retaining more than 25%.

The average person speaks at a rate of about 125 words per minute. Our brains, however, have the capacity to understand over 400 words per minute. This means we are using only 25% of our listening ability. Is it any wonder that with all that extra time available our minds wander?

During those brief pauses in a discussion or presentation our minds move on to other topics than the one at hand. We can be planning our trip home, holidays, our new car, a golf game, a play etc. during that time that has been allowed to us. It's important for speakers to remember this and make adjustments so they don't lose their audiences.

Participation and Feedback

One way to reduce wandering is for speakers to increase their verbal speed. Regularly and often refocusing the attention of the listener is helpful, as is seeking audience participation or colleague feedback during the delivery of the message. Later, find out what listeners thought of the presentation and take their feedback to heart. Was the discussion or speech difficult to follow? Too long or too boring?

Taking Notes for Future Reference

Encourage listeners to take notes.

We cannot possibly remember every conversation, telephone call, instruction or presentation we participate in each day. Whether you're caring for a patient, cleaning a room, sitting in a meeting, or attending a lecture you should take notes to help you become a more effective employee or parent.

If you get into the habit of reviewing your notes at the end of the day you can use the information for planning the next day. Your efficiency will improve rapidly. Taking notes also demonstrates you respect the speaker.

We like to be recognized and listened to and by taking notes, we're telling the person communicating with us that we value what they have to say. I suggest you use an electronic device of some kind to record your notes daily. Having such a record becomes invaluable to you should you wish to review your activities over any time period.

Reasons for Listening

The following list shows that good listening habits can do much for us in our personal and work lives, including:

- Helping us fully understand work expectations
- Demonstrating we're productive and valued employees
- Improving our rapport with our co-workers, managers and clients
- Better resolving problems with other staff, patients and other clients
- Answering questions we may have
- Showing support and respect of others
- Helping us win friends
- Solving mutual problems
- Developing confidence
- Providing time to think before asking questions
- Reaching better and more informed decisions

These skills are the foundation of your future successes. They are easy to understand and you will start seeing positive results in your life from the first time you start applying them at home and at work.

A common characteristic of every one of the "Heroes" in our book, Heroes in the Halls, is that they each have the characteristic of being strong effective communicators. Whether it is listening to clients and patients, discussions with colleagues, issuing or receiving instructions, interpreting situations or results, our "Heroes" have excellent listening and communicating skills, and are respected for them.

They set the example for their teams, bring them together to meet and plan daily, weekly, and long-term activities, and are constantly visible to their team members.

CHAPTER HIGHLIGHTS

- Why are good communication and listening skills so important for your future success?

- Name 5 factors which contribute to successful communications.

- Name 5 factors which cause poor communications.

- What are several of the requirements of being a good listener?

- What are some of the reasons for listening to others, and what can we gain from the practice?

Chapter Ten
Identifying Leaders

During her 16 years as a practical nurse, our hero, Roxana, has gained an excellent understanding of what makes good leaders and leadership. She feels that she, like many other staff within most organizations, could contribute more to their organizations if given the opportunity, and time to do so. She is convinced that further staff involvement in departmental and corporate leadership could lead to much more engaged and trusting work environments. Roxana is often recognized for her excellent delivery of services to her patients and the fact that she is well-organized at all times. She feels that all leaders must be visible within their departments and organizations, at all times, and be totally aware of the functions of each staff member.

This chapter on leadership reflects the skills, talents, passions, and empathy embraced by our modern day Heroes in the Halls. As we begin, I would like you to visualize the large TV screen in your brain. This is an analogy we used in the visioning chapter to bring the concept to life. As you visualize, consider your past life and individuals you would consider to have led you in the past.

Go back to your childhood, elementary school, middle school, high school, and college to define the qualities and characteristics of leaders you have known. What did they do that stands out? Think it through. Were they caring, patient, trustworthy, fun, good planners, and good coaches? Did they have the ability to recognize you and those around you as having certain talents, and did they truly care about you?

Finally, did they listen to you and respect your thoughts and ideas? Is it possible these leaders in your life's history could be your personal heroes?

Now think about past leaders you have known and write down their qualities and behaviors. Should you be in a group setting at this time, compare your notes with those of your colleagues. Together, identify ten characteristics all team members had on their lists. Each team member should describe the involvement they had with the leaders they identified and how the leadership trait was demonstrated. As you complete this process, you'll discover that you've developed your own personal leadership concept and you'll start to understand how your actual past experiences have shaped this concept.

Based on extensive research and having personally taught at least five thousand students on the topic of leadership during my career, I have developed the following list of what leaders of excellence provide for those they lead. I encourage you to read this list carefully and ask yourself whether the characteristics defined are ones you already possess, or are some you need to work on developing. Keep the list of leadership traits you need to strengthen as a set of targets for the upcoming year. Finally, besides what is contained in this book, do your own research and expand your leadership skill levels. You'll soon find they'll lead to new opportunities in the future.

Characteristics of Great Leaders

- **Visionaries**: Have the ability to see and know where they want to go or where to guide their team.

- **Contact Developers**: often exchange information, help others solve problems, and assist others in efforts to be more effective. Example: A leader who has developed a new methodology for cleaning patient rooms would share that system with other colleagues to facilitate greater efficiency within their organization. In turn, leaders are open to learning specific operational areas others are doing effectively.

- **Passionate**: a continual excitement and dedication to work and a determined drive to do the best possible job with the resources available. Leaders like what they do and are proud of their work.

- **Highly Involved**: link with others through communicative processes rather than working in a vacuum. Working as a team, answers to most issues are readily decided. If you can provide a vision of what it is you would like to achieve, a team's power can guide you to that destination quickly.

- **Learners**: constantly seeking new information about improved processes, which not only makes them more valuable as individuals, but also enables them to become more effective teachers, employees, and employers.

- **Trustworthy**: reliable, honest, someone to believe in who would not take advantage of you, and someone who would support you without question.

More on Trust

At this time in our business world there is a tremendous lack of trust, due to poor economic conditions, poor communication practices, a lack of care for colleagues, and a reluctance to share. As a leader, you have the power to start improving trust levels. Talk to your colleagues about it and do something—action is required to change environments and mindsets. One excellent trust exercise is to suggest to your team they define what the word "trust" means to them individually. Take those findings and combine them for a team discussion, then prioritize the most frequently mentioned characteristics and use those four or five of them as the standard for your team.

New Supervisors and Managers

It's likely that those reading this book will have an opportunity at some point in the future to advance within their organization to a supervisory or leadership role. Being new to the role will require developing personal traits to ensure you grow into an effective leader who is well-received and respected by those under your guidance.

- **Reputation:** You must be credible and able to generate trust, and be known as a person of good character whose practice is to do the right thing.

- **Competent:** New leaders must be confident and skilful in their roles in order for them to gain the respect of their staff.

- **Humble:** It's important that a new leader isn't perceived as someone who knows everything. Leaders should show that they have the wisdom to ask colleagues for help. "Meetings of the Minds" could be held to allow staff to develop solutions to problems. These are a powerful way to receive practical information and portray you as a leader at the same time.

- **Influential:** All leaders, new and experienced, must demonstrate that they have the skillsets to guide others to achieve departmental and corporate goals.

- **Visible**: Being seen and available to staff is an important part of good leadership. Spending time with staff, observing, listening and providing advice, or answering questions lets people know you have an awareness of the department's needs and concerns.

What Makes Leaders Great?

During our lifetimes we have learned about many great leaders, people who have inspired change in countries and causes. They have protected people, made discoveries to better mankind, and left the world a better place. Further along I will provide examples of such leaders, but rest assured that leaders can be found on any scale. They aren't only hugely historical ones. Think about yourself today. Have you been leading, following, or coasting? Is your department better because of your leadership and input? Do you take time for your colleagues and patients, even to the point of becoming familiar with their families?

Along those same lines, remember that great leaders do not neglect their own families. To this end, have you created a balance in your life that makes home a happy, nurturing place? All of these are examples of leadership that only you control. Do know that it is absolutely possible for you to do so. Let's look at two or three leaders who have set the standard for what leadership is all about globally, and briefly review their stories:

Jonas Salk

Dr. Salk was a physician and medical researcher who developed the first safe vaccine for polio. He was born in 1914 in New York City to a poor family that was dedicated to having Jonas educated. In 1939 he earned his medical degree and soon after began a fellowship to the University of Michigan, where he commenced working on developing a flu vaccine. In 1947, he went to the University of Pittsburgh and began research on polio. In 1955 when the vaccine was approved for general use, Salk became a national hero and was given a special citation at the White House by President Dwight D. Eisenhower. The vaccine had a dramatic impact on the disease, with cases dropping from 57,000 in the US to 1,000 a decade later. Dr. Salk went on to study disease like multiple sclerosis and cancer. He died in 1996.

Nelson Mandela

Nelson Mandela, another true hero, was a leader in the 1940s of both peaceful protests and armed resistance activities against the white minorities' oppressive regime of apartheid in South Africa. He was arrested by the minority government and imprisoned for nearly 30 years but still became the leader for the eradication of apartheid both in South Africa and globally. He was released from jail in 1990 and in 1994 became the first black President of South Africa, forming a multi-ethnic government to oversee the country's transition. He was champion for human rights, peace, and social justice in his own nation and around the world. Nelson Mandela died in 2013 at the age of 95.

John Fitzgerald Kennedy

John F Kennedy became the 35th President of the United States in 1961. He came from a very wealthy family and attended prestigious schools, including Harvard and Princeton. He was a talented writer but never excelled in school. Elected to the U.S. Senate in 1952, he went on to defeat Richard Nixon by a narrow margin in 1960. At age 43 Jack Kennedy was the second youngest person ever to hold the office of President of the United States.

During his Presidency Kennedy experienced major challenges and successes. These included the Peace Corps movement across the globe and the disastrous Bay of Pigs invasion in Cuba in 1961. He was a champion for civil rights later in his term, sending a civil rights bill to Congress in 1963 that eventually passed as the landmark Civil Rights Act in 1964.

On November 21, 1963 the President flew to Dallas, Texas for a campaign event. The following day he and Governor Connally rode through downtown Dallas where the President was assassinated by 24-year-old warehouse worker, Lee Harvey Oswald. President Kennedy was shot twice and died shortly thereafter at the age of 46.

Kennedy is considered a hero, and one of the most beloved Presidents of the USA. The most memorable image of the Kennedy Presidency is that of Camelot, the idyllic castle of legendary King Arthur. As his wife Jackie said after his death, "There will be great presidents again but there'll never be another Camelot."[4]

A Dedication to All Heroes in the Halls

Is there really any difference between heroes Salk, Mandela, and Kennedy, and ourselves and the heroes we work with? I think not! The three men did influence their countries, millions of people, and the world in general, but our hundreds of thousands of employee heroes also influence millions of individuals worldwide. Looking at the qualities of all the leaders discussed we could say that all heroes have certain characteristics. Among these are:

- Vision
- Communication Skills
- Courage

- Commitment
- Belief in Self
- Passion
- Empathy
- Experience
- Knowledge
- Energy

Earlier in this chapter we discussed several characteristics of leaders as well. All leadership qualities and characteristics we have discussed can be found within ourselves, our organizations, and our teams. This is why the talent we have available today is incredible; members of staff must consider themselves unique and talented to help those we care for and work with. We know that every one of our day-to-day heroes can do so much more for themselves and others once they seize the opportunity to do so together. That is our challenge...and it can be done!

Dave Frohnmayer, former president of my alma mater, The University of Oregon, died Monday, March 2, 2015. He left us a message which is relevant to all of our Heroes in the Halls:

"I grew up with a real sense that an individual can make a difference, and that, if you can, you should." We can all make differences! We can all be leadership heroes![5]

CHAPTER HIGHLIGHTS

- What are some of the characteristics of leaders you have known, and have influenced your life?

- How can an ineffective leader influence us personally and departmentally?

- What do you feel are some the qualities required for you to become a successful leader now, and in the future?

- What are at least five of the characteristics required by leaders of excellence?

Endnotes

[1] Reference from publication "Great Britain Health and Safety Executive" article "Work Related Stress, Anxiety and Depression Studies" 2014-2015

[2] Reference from article in the Springer Age publication regarding the "FLAME STUDY (Finnish Longitudinal Study of Municipal Employees)" published online November 7, 2014

[3] Quote from a company article written for his company "The Success Motivation Institute"

[4] Quotation by Jacqueline Kennedy in the publication "The CAMELOT Interview" Life Magazine December 6, 1963

[5] As written in the University of Oregon Alumni Magazine, March 2015

About the Author

Claude Halpin was born in Calgary, Alberta, where he attended elementary and high school. He graduated from Mount Royal College, in Calgary, with a diploma in Business Administration before attending the University of Oregon, in Eugene, Oregon, where he received his Bachelor of Science degree in Business Administration (BSc). He then enrolled at the University of Toronto and received his two-year diploma in Hospital Administration (DHA).

During his career he has gained extensive experience as the Chief Executive Officer of three major Canadian health care facilities, ranging from 270 to 2,000 beds in Alberta and Ontario, providing acute care, rehabilitation, and long-term care services.

As a consultant he has worked with all levels of corporate leadership and board governance, providing services involving organizational reviews, leadership programs, development of more effective organizational teams and strategic planning.

He has held teaching appointments on the faculties of the Universities of Alberta, Otttawa and Toronto.

In collaboration with the Ontario Hospital Association, Claude developed the first "Effective Governance Program" in Canada, and delivered the program to over 1,600 board members from approximately 200 hospitals and health care organizations.

He developed Leadership programs-"Leading in the New Millenium, I and II," and "Leading through Exemplary Leadership I and II." These programs in collaboration with the OHA were attended by thousands of participants over several years.

Mr. Halpin co-facilitated the Physician Management Institute IV on the topics of Stress and Change Management for hundreds of leading Canadian physicians for the Canadian Medical Association. He was also an accreditation officer for several years.

Mr. Halpin has conducted almost 2,300 individual behavioral diagnostics, using the Thomas Behavioral System. He has used the program extensively in his Executive Recruitment, individual, and team development practice.

Mr. Halpin believes passionately in the talents, and power, of the individual and feels that every organization can become stronger, and more successful, when they concentrate on recognizing the potential of their people.